The Forward Book of Poetry
2016

This anthology was designed and produced by Forward Worldwide, which also supports the Prizes. Forward Worldwide is a leading content marketing agency based in London, Shanghai and Singapore. Forward develops digital products and creates engaging, shareable content in multiple languages, raising brand awareness and driving sales. Clients include Patek Philippe, American Express, Standard Life, Fidelity, B&Q and Tesco. Find us at forwardww.com and @tweetfwd

The Forward Book of Poetry
2016

FORWARD
Worldwide

LONDON

First published in Great Britain by
Forward Worldwide · 83 Clerkenwell Road · London ECIR 5AR
in association with
Faber & Faber · Bloomsbury House · 74-77 Great Russell Street
London WCIB 3DA

ISBN 978 0 571 32538 2 (paperback)

Printed and bound by CPI Group (UK) · Croydon CRO 4YY

A CIP catalogue reference for this book
is available at the British Library.

To Joanna Mackle
with love and thanks

Contents

Highly Commended Poems 2015

Foreword

WELCOME TO THIS ANTHOLOGY of poems published in the UK and Ireland between the autumns of 2014 and 2015. It's been my pleasure to chair the panel judging the Forward Prizes this year and I have been delighted by my fellow judges' attention to technical detail and their scrutiny of form and function, passion and risk.

We – Colette Bryce, Carrie Etter, Emma Harding, Warsan Shire and I – were looking for writers who weren't simply talking to themselves, or to the poetry community. We were looking for poets who were reaching out, testing themselves against complex subjects, being happily challenged by the demands of simplicity and the pressure to be both beautiful and clear. This anthology is the result.

The arts in the UK seem always to be apologising for themselves, having to remind funders, publishers, politicians, media outlets and all the complicated machinery of commercial reproduction that they still have value. Within that already-embattled scene, poetry has seemed an endangered species for decades. Yet poetry continues and even thrives, in spite of reduced shelf-space, culled author lists and the near-impossibility of earning a living as a poet. It may not be enjoyable to practise a craft that is often less than commercially viable, but the work here shows how many poets can build a creative life nonetheless and exploit the freedom their non-viability grants them.

Poetry is an art with the power to remind us of all that is inherently valuable. Pricing these things – thoughts, touches, instants of animal awareness – would be, to say the least, discourteous. Celebrating the details of our lives and worlds, honouring them, remembering their loss, grieving and raging and speaking for them – this is what poetry can do extremely well. This is what we were looking for as we read.

For as long as our arts can insist on being as remarkable as possible – potentially life-changing interventions for individual hearts and minds – then they will survive, they will be worthy of the love and support they need to flourish. Their continuance is necessary because it means they will be able to keep on serving their audiences as they should – reminding us of our humanity, saving us in our dark times, encouraging us, giving us more ways to be more ourselves, showing us the humanity of others and the irreplaceability of every moment, every breath.

So we were looking for excellence.

And we weren't easily pleased. We found a number of writers who weren't quite in control of prose as a poetic medium and a greater number of writers who might have been served by more critical, or perhaps more patient, editing. It was disheartening to read work that could have reached its fullest potential with just one more pause for breath, a chance for one last pass.

Still, we were exhilarated to read experienced writers pushing their abilities. And it's very clear that a wonderfully vibrant new generation of poets is emerging. The idea of what a poem is and can be is returning to old forms and creating new ones. You'll come across a pantoum here, sonnets, true prose poetry and a whole variety of free verse, shaped to the needs of each subject, necessary and beautiful.

We were also heartened to read so many different sources of material: from sport, to film and photography to political outrage, illness, and annealed grief. Poets working today are both radical and confident in poetry's ability to range, borrow and explore. More and more varied voices are clearly engaging with poetry as a condensed, precise and hugely emotive means of expression. Landscapes and creatures aren't simply holding up beauty to the keen observing eye, there is a layering of meaning and narrative, a crafting of significance. History is blending with evolution, with industrialisation, with rumours of war and deep wounds, long held silent.

Amongst our best practitioners, poetry is currently held to be an appropriate medium for the discussion and exploration of anything and everything – just as it should be.

What you'll find here are – we believe – the best poems of 2015, some taken from this year's shortlisted collections, with still more highly commended pieces. If you're a poet, you'll find a great deal here to warm and inspire: technically skilful writing, more fluid approaches – unleashed emotion and controlled epiphanies. There are also journeys along the border – incautious travellers beware – between quality poetry and quality prose.

If you love poetry already then we're confident that you'll be pleased and troubled and tickled and haunted by the ghost of a song, the beauty in a housing estate stairwell, by tumults of fruits, unstarred nights, the courtesy of little goats – all the generosity of creation and the unblinking attention that you'd expect.

If you know someone who might be ready for poetry, or who's drifted away from it, a reader you would like to please with news from poetry's present and signs of its vigorous future, then I would recommend that you should send them this. Give them this. Slip this into their hand with our blessing and our thanks to every author included.

AL Kennedy, June 2015

Preface

SOMETIMES ALL IT TAKES IS A JOKE. The announcement of the 2015
Forward Prizes shortlists broke on Twitter with seven flip words.

Poetry pantheon cracks open. No one injured. #forwardprizes

Behind that tweet lay 185 poetry collections, 227 single poems – and
a sense of astonishment that started in an airy room in Clerkenwell,
where five judges were charged with choosing the best contemporary
poetry published in the UK and Ireland.

Before they thrashed out the shortlists for the three Forward Prizes
for Best Collection, Best First Collection and Best Single Poem, they
were gently reminded that I founded the awards nearly 25 years ago
with just two aims: to celebrate excellence in poetry and to increase
its audience.

Some might hear this as an instruction to play safe, but the writer
AL Kennedy, flanked by radio producer Emma Harding and poets
Colette Bryce, Carrie Etter and Warsan Shire, clearly believed readers,
even those new to poetry, deserve to be surprised.

They felt these readers – you – can cope with unfamiliar names, with
forms that resemble prose or drama more closely than canonical 'poetry'
and with subjects more often raised in news bulletins than in literary
discussions. The poems they valued contain references that range from
Zinedine Zidane and Venus Williams to Irish nuns, from Chinese food
and Polish migration to gay marriage and the inevitability of rain.

It has been grand to see the BBC and the *Guardian*, among others,
lead their reports on the 2015 Forward shortlists by rejoicing that major
poetry publishers' lists are no longer entirely, or almost entirely, devoid
of black, Asian or minority ethnic writers, as they were ten years ago.

It's good too that the Best First Collection shortlist features three
books by first- and second-generation immigrants to Britain. It was
sobering to note that the Forward Prize for Best Collection has, in 23
years, been awarded only four times to a woman. Kei Miller, last year's
winner, was the first non-white recipient. Change, deep change within
the publishing world, is overdue.

And yet, while several shortlistees make their multiple identities –
Sikh, Chinese, American, Irish, British – a feature of their work, others
prefer not to. One in particular has such a horror of publicity that his

picture cannot be found on the internet and even his publisher knows next to nothing about him. The curious should glance at the biographies at the back of this book, but I shall call him 'A'.

His unfashionable reticence raises questions: should poets' identities – the tags marked 'race', 'ethnicity', 'gender' – dominate all conversation about their writing? And if so, what space is left for that which cannot be easily labelled and so remains invisible?

I don't know the answer, nor even if there is an answer. I do know, however, that when considering poems selected from five judges' readings of 185 new collections and 227 single poems, it's impossible to generalise – and equally impossible not to try. Anyone attempting to categorise this year's poetry crop will need a vast supply of labels.

Among the authors of the 50-odd highly commended poems that compose the second part of this book, there are writers such as Kate Tempest who attract passionate crowds, and others, such as Clive James, whose fans extend far beyond poetry. Some are impresarios: combining influential posts as professors, editors and judges with an apparently effortless ability to spot the talents of the future. Take a bow: Don Paterson, Sean O'Brien, George Szirtes. Others – one thinks again of 'A' – are household names only in their own homes.

They have this in common. Their work pleased enough of the judges to earn a place in this book – and we hope, therefore, that they will please you too.

Thank you to Georgie Hopton, the artist responsible for this year's stunning cover design. Hopton is the third in a distinguished sequence of contemporary artists – following Michael Craig-Martin and Gary Hume – to support the Forward Prizes with their art. We owe them gratitude for deepening the big conversation about poetry and bringing it to new eyes and ears.

Thank you to the Forward Worldwide team, especially Will Scott, Casey Jones, Christopher Stocks, Sarah Bolwell and Karen Heaney. Without the long-standing and loyal support of Forward Worldwide, sponsors since the start, the Forward books and Prizes would not exist.

Felix Dennis, who for years sponsored the prize for Best First Collection, has continued his generosity posthumously: we thank his executors. We have long wished to give something to the runners-up

in this category: thanks to the Wingate Foundation, the five Best
First Collection poets have each been offered commissions to write a
new poem on the National Poetry Day 2015 theme of Light. Look
for them on the Forward Arts Foundation website.

The strategic thinking, fund-raising, creative and audience
development skills of Rebecca Blackwood and Clare Cumberlidge of
Thirteen Ways have enabled the Forward Arts Foundation to grow
and change, embedding both the Prizes and National Poetry Day into
the nation's cultural life. We look forward to our new partnership with
them delivering poetry in surprising and high profile ways to the public
realm of the nation. Thank you to Emily Cropton for her design support
in the development of the book.

Arts Council England, the John Ellerman Foundation, Esmée Fairbairn
Foundation and Rothschild Foundation all make our work possible.

Our trustees, Nigel Bennett, Joanna Mackle, Robyn Marsack, Giles
Spackman and Martin Thomas, have been tireless in turning the Forward
Arts Foundation's dreams into reality.

Finally, thank you to the staff of the Forward Arts Foundation,
Susannah Herbert and Maisie Lawrence.

William Sieghart, *June 2015*

Shortlisted Poems
The Forward Prize for Best Collection

Ciaran Carson

In Memory

As he told it
when the boy
he was stumbled
on the well
in the derelict brickyard
deep as a brick mill chimney
leaning over the rim
he shouted
the two syllables
of his name
deep down into it
to hear his echo.
Now that the man
he would become
is dead
that unfathomable
darkness
echoes
still.

The Blotting-paper

He opened a book
he hadn't opened for years
a sheet of blotting-paper fell
from between its leaves
it looked like the map of a city
whose streets petered out into blank
or led into blot
overwritten with false beginnings
and no real endings;
and he tried to remember the hour
he first had lost himself
in that labyrinth of words once almost
decipherable by
the mirror in the dim hallway
of a house no longer
on the map.

Eiléan Ní Chuilleanáin

THE WORDS COLLIDE

The scribe objects. You can't put it like that,
I can't write that. But the client
is a tough small woman forty years old.
She insists. She needs her letter
to open out full of pleated revolving silk
and the soft lobes of her ears
where she flaunts those thin silver wires.

She wants to tell her dream to the only one
who will get the drift. How she saw their children lying
every one dressed out in their simple fears. They glowed,
the shape of their sentence outlined in sea green.
Among those beloved exiles
one sighed happy, as a curtain
lightened and the grammar changed, and the wall
showed pure white in the shape of a bird's wing.

But when she whispered it to the scribe he frowned
and she saw she had got it wrong, she had come
to a place where they all spoke the one language:
it rose up before her like a quay wall
draped in sable weeds. He said,
You can't put those words into your letter.
It will weigh too heavy, it will cost too much,
it will break the strap of the postman's bag,
it will crack his collarbone. The bridges
are all so bad now, with that weight to shift
he's bound to stumble. He'll never make it alive.

Dream Shine

When I switch off the light
the darkness lasts only
an instant, they appear

like women in their doorways
hesitant, brandishing
their dim lamp. The shine

reflected from deep snow
edges the darkness
of a hanging gown,

singles out a surface,
a beam sliding upwards,
a gleam suspended;

a slice wriggles up
from a fountain in the courtyard,
slips into the room,

finds itself a shelf,
bobs beside it –
who would not prefer

to sleep surrounded
by these gentle intruders,
wrapped in their whispers:

Go to sleep, dream about
the mouse that used to watch you,
looking out from his door

in the dashboard, sidelong,
as soon as the engine growled
and the car moved on its road?

Paul Muldoon

PELT

Now rain rattled
the roof of my car
like holy water
on a coffin lid,
holy water and mud
landing with a thud

though as I listened
the uproar
faded to the stoniest
of silences... They piled
it on all day
till I gave way

to a contentment
I'd not felt in years,
not since that winter
I'd worn the world
against my skin,
worn it fur side in.

Cuba (2)

I'm hanging with my daughter in downtown Havana.
She's worried people think she's my mail-order bride.
It might be the *Anseo* tattooed on her ankle.
It might be the tie-in with that poem of mine.

The '59 Buicks. The '59 Chevys.
The '59 Studebakers with their whitewalled wheels.
The rain-bleached streets have been put through a mangle.
The sugar mills, too, are feeling the squeeze.

We touch on how Ireland will be inundated
long before the nil-nil draw.
Che Guevara's father was one of the Galway Lynches.
Now a genetically engineered catfish can crawl

on its belly like an old-school guerrilla.
Maybe a diminished seventh isn't the note
a half-decent revolution should end on?
The poor with their hands out for "pencils" and "soap"?

Hopped up though I am on caffeine
I've suffered all my life from post-traumatic fatigue.
Even a world-class sleeper like Rip Van Winkle
was out of it for only twenty years.

A fillet of the fenny
cobra may yet fold into a blood-pressure drug.
A passion for marijuana
may yet be nipped in the bud.

Some are here for a nose job. Some a torn meniscus.
The profits from health tourism have been salted away.
The blue scorpion takes the sting from one cancer.
Ovarian may yet leave us unfazed.

Hemingway's sun hat is woven from raffia.
He's tried everything to stop the rot.
He's cut everything back to the bare essentials.
His '55 Chrysler's in the shop.

We'll sit with Hemingway through yet another evening
of trying to stay off the rum.
I'm running down the list of my uncles.
It was Uncle Pat who was marked by a gun.

Our friends Meyer Lansky and the Jewish mafia
built the Riviera as a gambling club.
Had it not been for the time differential
Uncle Arnie might have taken a cut.

The best baseball bats are turned from hibiscus.
They're good against people who get in your way.
The best poems, meanwhile, give the answers
to questions only they have raised.

We touch on Bulat and Yevgeny,
two Russian friends who've since left town.
The Cuban ground iguana
is actually quite thin on the ground.

The cigars we lit up on Presidents' Avenue
have won gold medals in the cigar games.
Now it seems a cigar may twinkle
all the more as the light fails.

My daughter's led me through Hemingway's villa
to a desk round which dusk-drinkers crowd.
She insists the *Anseo* on her Achilles tendon
represents her being in the here and now.

The cattle egret is especially elated
that a plow may still be yoked to an ox.

Others sigh for the era of three-martini lunches
and the Martini-Henry single-shot.

When will we give Rothstein and Lansky and their heavies
the collective heave?
In Ireland we need to start now to untangle
the rhetoric of 2016.

The Riviera's pool is shaped like a coffin.
So much has been submerged here since the Bay of Pigs.
Maybe that's why the buildings are wrinkled?
Maybe that's why the cars have fins?

Claudia Rankine

THE NEW THERAPIST SPECIALIZES...

The new therapist specializes in trauma counseling. You have only ever spoken on the phone. Her house has a side gate that leads to a back entrance she uses for patients. You walk down a path bordered on both sides with deer grass and rosemary to the gate, which turns out to be locked.

At the front door the bell is a small round disc that you press firmly. When the door finally opens, the woman standing there yells, at the top of her lungs, Get away from my house! What are you doing in my yard?

It's as if a wounded Doberman pinscher or a German shepherd has gained the power of speech. And though you back up a few steps, you manage to tell her you have an appointment. You have an appointment? she spits back. Then she pauses. Everything pauses. Oh, she says, followed by, oh, yes, that's right. I am sorry.

I am so sorry, so, so sorry.

In Line At The Drugstore…

In line at the drugstore it's finally your turn, and then it's not as he walks in front of you and puts his things on the counter. The cashier says, Sir, she was next. When he turns to you he is truly surprised.

Oh my God, I didn't see you.

You must be in a hurry, you offer.

No, no, no, I really didn't see you.

Peter Riley

Due North, Part VIII

(Nicholas Ludford. Derek Bailey. Restlessness And Serenity.
and leaps across full ditches.)

Wandering all over Europe very much at home
talking singing from shore to shore
gathering the daylight, long straight forest edges
like black cliffs, paths out of the backs of
suburban housing estates across abandoned
coal mine sites, miles of telegraph posts and electricity pylons
          some with kestrels' or storks' nests on them.

The lines bend to the ground at points of regret *For all I rue
and I rue and I rue*   (she turns her face towards)

Migrant workers, Jewish artists who fled central Europe
longing for home, old or new, remembering the particulars,
       the forms and colours of molehills in the family meadow
       The lonely desert-man sees the tents of the happy tribes
           "Man with brother Man to meet,
           And as a brother kindly greet" words
           past nations / public words
           distant hopes / whispered in the night,
           far from the ken of the broadcasters.

           "Horo Mhairi dhu, turn ye to me" (in the dance)
(in the dialect) an almost silent message threaded
from shore to shore by mountain and valley
corner shops and multi-storey car-parks, a sustained
assurance that silences the amplifiers.

           Everywhere embarrassed and humiliated
           everywhere alien
           where in the world can I moor my heart

> but in the long moors of the north,
> heather and brown earth under which
> the murdered children lie

Turn, speak to me if you can, whisper in earth tones
remind me of the optimism of the infant
and how it will grow, if not arrested,
into an extended speech, a moral vocabulary
to defend the civic concept, the width of society
crowded with dialects freed from comedy / we do not steal.

He walks in covered in splashes of cow-dung and says, "You seem, Mrs W., to reprimand Wordsworth for not writing in a thick Cumberland dialect…"

He walks in covered in smears of axle-grease and says, "You seem to think, Mr A., that the northernness from which you gain your fame and fortune, is a bit of a joke…"

First riposte to Judith Butler
> The "I" in the mode of knowing, knows
> its own vulnerability, and thus others'.

Second riposte to Judith Butler
> It would seem that all the persons that constitute me,
> some here, others mourned, unknown, not even the
> name, lost sight of in the northern tracts, it seems
> they all consolidate into the simple, unique thing:
> speech visage and name, "I", the only one of these
> things finally capable of thought and act.

The strongest among us feels the pangs of failure
when the latest human lapse
flashes onto the screen, far beyond thought
> and the great performer loses his place in the script.

We are that faltering tribe, crouched in the sand,
waiting for the bombers to pass over.
Rising into narrative "I" is again "we", the lament
takes up again the living-spaces of the territory
caught up in guitar tones and 6v polyphony the song
grows into history. We follow it we trace it
on the curve of the motorway arm the red procession
we follow wherever it goes

For we are permanent.
We have permanent smiles and permanent frowns.
The shining in the night, in the glass towers, is also us,
the force that jumps the white fuse, the precept.
When the tension is too much we complain
in night whispers, arm across arm

Our past works buried in sand, a glazed brick waiting
for an archaeologist, too late – scrubbed clean and
lovingly contemplated, on show to the nations
but we have gone our ways into the lost trails.
        Tower of Blue Horses (too late)
        "the generation that squandered its poets" too late now
        oh it's too late now, Radnóti sinks into the mud, Jobbik
        (they could get 20%)
        speaks openly of imprisoning the gypsies.
        Should have thought of this earlier. If the left
        had deigned to participate in practical politics some
        time in the last 60 years we might still have
        a socialism worth voting for.

The big songs thought of this and wrapped it up. The largest sense
of person walked and talked it across the earth long before, and
                                       something
constructed from an entire life at that point was set on the ground
to include hope in a realism at a moral pace, an insistence,
a sufficient apple in the old red hand, but it never happened.
The big song turned inwards on itself.

The small song whispered itself over the Atlantic Ocean
with the emigrants, bounced back as clear as a bell
and become unstoppable / Mansoul glides over the water
   the little song balances itself on a light tread,
   antitheses and repetitions, a chime
   at the turning of anybody's life

               The grandfather's song, singing
               the greatest possible particularity
               into the greatest possible unity
               immanent tones of the world
               constantly returning home
               where the small hands reach.

There are only long-term answers.
            The lament is full-throated.
            The linnet is falling thought
                  from across the world
                  landing on the ground
                  shouting
                     O Spring, come!
                     Open! Grow! Twitter!

and then adiós.

            Amor, muerte: I
shall elicit a lot of caring
            from your mental lips
en tus brazos me durmiera
            y la vida no quitarte
body or soul
            yo soy un hombre correcto / sincero
            and have things to be made known

            For the siren
            finally convinced me
                  que es muy bonita

and there will be a long peace
on the earth's sutures

the fluttering butterflies
the rusting battleships
in the harbour.

Shortlisted Poems
The Felix Dennis Prize for
Best First Collection

Mona Arshi

THE LION

How unstable and old he is now.
    Lion, like God, has snacks sent up

by means of a pulley. Although
    you can never master the deep language

of Lion, I am made dumb by the rough
    stroke of his tongue upon mine.

Nowadays I make allowances. We lie
    together and I hear the crackle of his bones

and when I bring myself to open my eyes
    he weeps, his pupils resembling dark

embroidered felt circles. Sometimes
    I think all I am is a comfort blanket for his

arthritic mouth. But many evenings he'll sit
    twisted behind the drapery solving my

vulgar fractions with nothing but his claws.
    Lion and I break bread; I tend to his mane and

he sets a thousand scented fuses under my skin.
    He starts undressing me under the sweetening stars.

Please girl, he mews; this might be the last time
    I will see how the thin light enters you.

WHAT EVERY GIRL SHOULD KNOW BEFORE MARRIAGE

after Sujata Bhatt

Eliminating thought verbs is the key to a successful marriage.

You're better off avoiding the reach for specificity and
curbing your interest in the interior of things.

The cobra always reverts to TYPE, tuneless
girls tend to wither on the vine.

Oil of jasmine will arouse river fish.

In the poetry of the Sung Dynasty the howling of monkeys
in gorges was used to express profound desolation.

Things you should have a good working knowledge
of: mitochondria, Roman roads, field glasses, making
rice (using the evaporation method only).

When your mother in law calls you smart,
it's not meant as a compliment.

The lighter her eyes, the further she'll travel.

Always have saffron in your kitchen cupboard
(but on no account ever use it).

*Taunt the sky during the day; the stars
will be your hazard at night.*

Do not underestimate the art of small talk. Learn some stock phrases such as 'they say Proust was an insufferable hypochondriac' or 'I'm confident that the Government will discharge their humanitarian obligations.'

Fasting sharpens the mind and is therefore a good time to practise reverse flight.

Your husband may not know you cheated with shop-bought *garam masala* but God will know.

Sarah Howe

(c) TAME

> 'It is more profitable to raise geese than daughters.'
> Chinese proverb

This is the tale of the woodsman's daughter. Born with a box
        of ashes set beside the bed,
in case. Before the baby's first cry, he rolled her face into the cinders –
        held it. Weak from the bloom
of too-much-blood, the new mother tried to stop his hand. He dragged
        her out into the yard, flogged her
with the usual branch. If it was magic in the wood, they never
        said, but she began to change:

her scar-ridged back, beneath his lashes, toughened to a rind; it split
        and crusted into bark. Her prone
knees dug in the sandy ground and rooted, questing for water,
        as her work-grained fingers lengthened
into twigs. The tree – a lychee – he continued to curse as if it
        were his wife – its useless, meagre
fruit. Meanwhile the girl survived. Feathered in greyish ash,
        her face tucked in, a little gosling.

He called her Mei Ming: *No Name*. She never learned to speak. Her life
        maimed by her father's sorrow.
For grief is a powerful thing – even for objects never conceived.
        He should have dropped her down
the well. Then at least he could forget. Sometimes when he set
        to work, hefting up his axe
to watch the cleanness of its arc, she butted at his elbow – again,
        again – with her restive head,

till angry, he flapped her from him. But if these silent pleas had
        meaning, neither knew.
The child's only comfort came from nestling under the
        lychee tree. Its shifting branches
whistled her wordless lullabies: the lychees with their watchful eyes,
        the wild geese crossing overhead.
The fruit, the geese. They marked her seasons. She didn't long to join
        the birds, if longing implies

a will beyond the blindest instinct. Then one mid-autumn, she craned
        her neck so far to mark the geese
wheeling through the clouded hills – it kept on stretching – till
        it tapered in a beak. Her pink toes
sprouted webs and claws; her helpless arms found strength
        in wings. The goose daughter
soared to join the arrowed skein: kin linked by a single aim
        and tide, she knew their heading

and their need. They spent that year or more in flight, but where –
        across what sparkling tundral wastes –
I've not heard tell. Some say the fable ended there. But those
        who know the ways of wild geese
know too the obligation to return, to their first dwelling place. Let this
        suffice: late spring. A woodsman
snares a wild goose that spirals clean into his yard – almost like
        it knows. Gripping its sinewed neck

he presses it down into the block, cross-hewn from a lychee trunk.
        A single blow. Profit, loss.

'Once there were...'
Cormac McCarthy

There were barnacles that marked the edges of oceans. Late scramblers on the rocks could feel their calcic ridges stoving sharply underfoot. The wet rocks glittered beneath and in the wind they smelled of verdigris. The barnacles fused in intricate settlements. For their whole lives they cleaved, and in turn the fragile rock cleaved to them. Volcanoes and thimbles and strange constellations. Together they mapped distant cities and willed the sea to overtake them. And when the russet tide came they opened themselves like unfamiliar lovers. The whole thing some actinic principle: a forest grew up in a second, to grace a world where the sun was a watery lamp. Where none had been before, white mouths frilled softly in the current and squat armour issued forth the unlikeliest of cilia: transparent, lightly haired, cherishing each updraft as, feathered, they moved with it. They only existed for that half-sunk terrain. And as they briefly lived, those tender quills wrote of their mystery.

Andrew McMillan

URINATION

I'm scared of bumping someone while they piss
those Mondays I'm a packhorse   bags hung
swinging around the urinal bodies
and one day   I know   I'll knock someone
and they'll piss their legs   or they'll turn slightly
and show another man their full arc
or they'll fall into their own wet puddle
cock limp   and neither of us will look
or he'll look at me avoiding looking
feigning interest in the hard cream tiles
maybe it's that I dream of being bumped
knocked from my aim by a stranger
the briefest touch during the private act
the toilet is an intimacy
only shared with parents when you are young
and once again when they are older
and with lovers when   say   on a Sunday
morning stretching into the bathroom
you wake to the sound of stream into bowl
and go to hug the naked body
stood with its back to you   and kiss the neck
and taste the whole of the night on there
and smell the morning's pale yellow loss
and take the whole of him in your hand
and feel the water moving through him
and knowing that this is love   the prone flesh
what we expel from the body and what we let inside

for the ones I never touched   for the ones
who wanted to watch films   who wanted
to talk   who wanted silence and said I
talked too much   for the one I saw
weeks after   laughing   for the one who served
me coffee and didn't recognise my hands
for the optimistic ones who write

their names on toilet walls   the ones
I never called   for the ones I called
who didn't answer   who left our love
suspended from the ceiling hooks
of that meatmarket city   for the ones
who left and settled down   the ones who wanted
knowledge   were curious   who gained something

from each encounter   used each other
who took what they needed   for everyone
they hurt   who felt burned out   the ones who
didn't realise everyone was burning
the ones who never slept   who died nightly
the ones who said they'd kill for it   for all of them
a gift   we were young   we only had our bodies

Matthew Siegel

'FOX GOES TO THE FOX HOSPITAL'

And look there he is back in the hospital
in the easy blue dressing gown, at this facility
with a delicate floral print on the walls.
He'd always had an affinity for flowers.
And healthy yet being repaired, he is back
in this gown and it is like an old costume
pulled out of a locked trunk in the attic
of bad dreams. In the gown he feels naked,
notices his softness, how his sex has never seemed less willing
to rise. As if there could be such a cause in this place.
He is healthy but writing a poem.
It is called 'going back to the hospital' and written
in lowercase, most notably the first person 'I'
which so often had stood properly capitalized
but for some reason today feels diminished.
He's writing a poem called 'going back to the hospital'
but really he wishes he could draw a comic
featuring a small mammal version of himself.
His animal would be a fox, he decides, and promptly
changes the title to 'fox goes to the fox hospital'.

Blood Work

The white sky presses a gauze pad
over my vein as the needle slips out.

The woman who draws from me smiles, always
remembers me, no matter how skinny I get.

No matter how dark the circles under my eyes,
she remembers me and how easy my veins are,

so visible, so thick, she doesn't even have to tie my arm,
but she does, and takes the smaller vein

the bigger one too easy. I don't tell her
the best to take my blood was a different woman

who used to draw blood from animals,
part the fur, find their blue tap and drain.

She lets me play with my filled tubes. *Can you feel
how warm they are? That's how warm you are inside*

and I nod, think about condoms, tissues
all the things that contain us but cannot.

Karen McCarthy Woolf

The Paperwork

I sit up in bed, try to make up my mind.
Will it change anything if I decide
your heart, liver, lungs, kidneys
are returned to the abdominal cavity?
My forefinger traces a path through
Option 5c: I understand these parts
will not be returned to their original position.

Your navel has not yet shrivelled,
each toenail is sacred.
Under *Other requests or concerns:*
hands, feet, face, hair—all must be left intact.
Brain to be restored to head, skin
stitched neatly and correctly.

I peer at the page on the doctor's lap.
Yes, they may saw through your breastbone,
but they'll sew your little tummy up
as if you were a rare mediaeval tapestry.
I'll make sure of that. *Eyes not to be touched.*
The doctor bites her lip, writes it in the box.

isn't really an office it's a cupboard with
no source of natural light, and I don't
realise it but I'm loved up like the other
mothers gazing at meconium as if it's fresh tar
on a road not an odourless, black shit
that's been on the boil for nine months and
Lydia, that's the registrar's name, she
gives me a paper cone of iced water from
the dispenser to calm me down and it
does calm me, the water flows through
me and now we're holding each other while
Simon's down in the mortuary and I tell
her all about how he lost his mother from
a brain tumour when I was six months
gone, how her name was Lydia too, that
it was so quick and now this.
We're still holding on when he comes back
then joins us in a circle of three and even
another form to fill in can't sober me up
as the morphine unpeels another mezzanine
of hell in a shopping centre where women
with rigid quiffs and rouged cheeks glide
up and down glass escalators and
people believe in the faux marble fountains
although it's all really a shimmering
colon. Anyway, I'm determined, I say,
as I leave the room, when I get out of here, if
it's the last thing I do, I *will* get you
a window because that's not right, expecting
someone to live and work and sign
death certificates without a window, no-one
should have to put up with that, it's not
right, she's a good person with
a good heart, she should have a window.

Shortlisted Poems
The Forward Prize for Best Single Poem

Maura Dooley

CLEANING JIM DINE'S HEART

In the afternoon sunlight at DeCordova sculpture park
she is on the top rung of a pair of steps cleaning a big
dark heart. And it has everything in it, this heart. Twice.
Even the coffee pot I brought back in hand luggage
that time, when such a thing was exotic, exciting,
more or less unknown. The coffee pot that blew up, in the end,
leaving its mark on the ceiling of Oakmead Road. That one.
Here it is, unthought of, unremembered, treacly, right here
in Jim Dine's big dark heart, which needs cleaning now,
front and back. Twice. Along with all its other secrets,
writ large, packed tight, here, in sunlight. His histories.
Which are our histories, some of them at least,
hands moving in darkness, worn-out shoes, rope,
the hammers and saws of a life together, coffee.
Caught forever here in a heartbeat and wiped clean now,
restored in afternoon sunlight, the darkness shining, made good.

Andrew Elliott

I once took my parents for lunch in a very expensive restaurant.
Dining at the table next to ours was Lucian Freud with a girl.
To begin with he stared at my mother who was even then
more beautiful than anyone else in the restaurant,
including the American actress at whom I made a point of not staring.

Then he turned his gaze on my father who in terms of self-obsession
could have taken Lucian Freud to the cleaners, passed him over,
taken his ticket, and come back the next day to collect him
like a camel's hair coat in cellophane. I felt for the girl
who was struggling. I could see she could see what was happening.

When our eyes met I winked and she laughed. She rolled
her eyes and I nodded. She had the kind of eyes which if eyes
were to be put into mass production would stream out of factories
in South Korea, and come in a choice of colours... My mother
for whom the meal was a treat was interested only in the actress.

My father was complaining as he always does about the food
to a waiter of skin and bone who may have been an artist himself,
starving for his art in a garret, only waiting to make ends meet,
the sparks to suddenly fly. I thought, *Him and that girl
should get together. She's thin like him. They'd be happy and be able*

to survive like freegans on what people like my father sent back...
Having already scraped his vegetables carefully onto a plate
on the side, my father was picking at his fish like a surgeon
trying to cut out a cancer. I thought of what all this was costing,
how children's eyes get everywhere dragging their minds behind them.

Meanwhile Freud had continued to stare and the novelty of someone
so famous staring at my father had worn off. It was embarrassing.
I'd a pea all ready on my fork to flick but when next I looked
their table had been cleared. The waiter was spreading a clean white
    cloth,
tugging it tight to the edges. With her eyes as much as anything else

my mother flashed, *She's leaving!* My father wanted pudding.

Ann Gray

My Blue Hen

I sing to my blue hen. I fold her wings
against my body. The fox has had her lover,
stealing through the rough grass,
the washed sky. I tell her, I am the blue heron
the hyacinth macaw. We have
a whispered conversation in French. I tell her
the horse, the ox, the lion, are all in the stars
at different times in our lives. I tell her there are
things even the sea can't do, like come in when
it's going out. I tell her my heart is a kayak
on wild water, a coffin, and a ship in full sail.
I tell her there is no present time,
an entire field of dandelions will give her
a thousand different answers. I tell her
a dog can be a lighthouse, a zebra finch can
dream its song, vibrate its throat while sleeping.
I tell her how the Mayan midwife sings each child
into its own safe song. Tonight, the moon holds back
the dark. I snag my hair on the plum trees. I tell her
I could've been a tree, if you'd held me here long enough.
I stroke her neck. She makes a bubbling sound,
her song of eggs and feathers. I tell her you were
a high note, a summer lightning storm of a man.

Claire Harman

The Mighty Hudson

> *'It's odd how they had the same name'*
> New York Star

After ten years of truck-work, he looked round and sighed:
Left a note for his nephew – 'The parts of my radio' –
And made for the city in a frilled shirt.

Found a walk-up full of the mythical skyline
With the river in front of it grey as a vein
And a tide running up into unreal suburbs.

Practised his weights on a fat co-lodger.
Lifting her one-handed up to the cobwebbed light.
Heard her hot geyser of giggling straight-faced but happy.

Arm-wrestled in bars with less effort than sighing,
Was bought beers by men who pincered his biceps.
Made friends with the barman. Got mystique by not smiling.

Enjoyed a short local career as a hero
After righting a load that got stuck on GW Bridge;
The newspaper posed him lifting a Merc into parking.

Soon after was called by Los Niños Non-Animal Circus
And shot to the top of the bill juggling three girls in lycra;
Their thighs left sequins stuck in his sideburns

And scents that perplexed him: one night he climbed onto their trailer,
Peeled back the roof like a ring-pull,
Picked Leonie out of her bunk through the skylight.

Didn't know his own strength, that's for certain.
Nor hers, when she struck with the whip, with the poker, the shotgun.
The lights of Jersey dimmed in the pith of his head

As he staggered back into the water, his namesake.
Keen as a mother to hurry him home.
Past the dark lighters, the bilge boats:

Past Peekskill, Poughkeepsie and Kingston.
Bear Mountain twirling oddly away like a girl.
The leaves blazing red as the fall, and the branches red too.

Kim Moore

And in that year my body was a pillar of smoke
and even his hands could not hold me.

And in that year my mind was an empty table
and he laid his thoughts down like dishes of plenty.

And in that year my heart was the old monument,
the folly, and no use could be found for it.

And in that year my tongue spoke the language
of insects and not even my father knew me.

And in that year I waited for the horses
but they only shifted their feet in the darkness.

And in that year I imagined a vain thing;
I believed that the world would come for me.

And in that year I gave up on all the things
I was promised and left myself to sadness.

And then that year lay down like a path
and I walked it, I walked it, I walk it.

Highly Commended Poems

Natalya Anderson

Clear Recent History

I was able to dance but not eat during the first stage
of my recovery. I wrote about this in a notebook
with a faded yellow construction paper cover. I took
daily class in studio G, which was broken into that night
you disappeared, the criminals having cracked parts
of the mirror. The next morning I made a mosaic while
warming up, arms raised in fifth position, head cocked

to examine the tiles of my neck. I was able to smoke
but not sleep during the second stage of my recovery.
I spoke about this into a tape recorder between assignments.
When I inhaled it was dusk; I went walking with a girl,
her Bull Terrier and her Doberman. The dogs ran into
the darkest patch of the field; we sat on cold wooden benches,
resting our heads against the fence's diamonds, separating

the streetlights' auburn halos. I was able to drink but not
kiss during the third stage of my recovery. I emailed my
friend about this every morning after my shift. The last
customers were leaning on cement, dipping crisp ends
into garlic mayonnaise. I enjoyed ice chimes, the dry cut
of vodka, while I wiped down the bar. I put my head on
my manager's chest; he held his rock glass in one hand
and the small of my back in the other. We hummed

a twilight mix. In the final stage of my recovery I was able
to decipher loving gestures. I texted my mother about this
while she was at the hair salon. My boyfriend's hands were
considerate. I was relieved when we married. I recognized
notes of lilac and tiger lily from the neighbour's garden just

after I gave birth. Filing my boy's certificate beneath
the staircase, I came across your final photograph. I crawled
out, held it up to the light, managed to squint, as if facing
thumbprints in the window which could be lathered away.

Sujata Bhatt

POPPIES IN TRANSLATION
for Ioana Ieronim

You tell us how in Romanian,
the wild poppies growing everywhere
are *a living flame of love* –

I imagine a single flame, and then a wildfire
by the roads, in the fields,
even between the railway tracks
where the sun spills through.

Windswept, they might be, these poppies,
        fluttering but confident,
                certain of love and life
as they grow in your poem, in Romanian.

As you speak, I remember those poppies;
as you speak, I imagine their thin, hairy stems
entangled with grass, and can simply feel
the way their wild redness
burns and reels: reckless, reckless with first love –
first sorrow and pain –   I can feel
the way light slides through their skins –
I have seen such poppies.
I have seen crêpe de chine, chiffon,
how their sheerest silks glisten in the sun,
bright as fresh blood.

They could be Hindu brides,
ripening in their red saris,
        as they face Agni –
skin glowing gold on gold on gold.

There are days when the poppies know something more.
Days when even in their restless trembling
            as the wind slaps down,
they ripple with the strength of their ragged petals.

I have seen such poppies:
What you call *a living flame of love*.
Even their stamens, whorls of black filaments,
ache with love – even their anthers,
powdered and smudged bluish black-violet,
                ache with love.

How else describe their power?

Still, in English, we don't know
        about this love.
Do we dare to say
        their intensity is love?

Who is the speaker in your poem?
Does she have the authority to make such claims?
What is it about your tone, your cadence,
that doesn't carry over into English?
Granted, we accept that *fire* and *flame*
describe more than colour;
granted, we understand strong emotions,
but adding *love* over here, *en passant*,
makes us uneasy.

In English, we say the poppies speak to us,
we say their intensity calls out to us –
and we say it's the urgency
of their *call* that moves us.

Why do we turn them into mouths?
About love we're not certain.
But it could be there, we say.
We can't exclude love,
and yet, we don't want to mention it.
That would be too much:
a living flame of love,
or even, *the intensity of the poppies' love* –
No, we say, no.
But the poppies do call us.

Kate Bingham

Heels

High over dogs and tricycles at the gate
I carried myself like wine in a wine glass

managing to avoid the usual huddles
of mums and dads

as instep to instep *left* and *right*
admired their patent leather reflections

proud and voluptuous still
after years in a box at the back of the wardrobe.

Nothing I had to celebrate but the shoes themselves
could account for such inappropriate footwear

and as I sank into the playground's spongy pink tarmac
even the littlest children knew it.

Jemma Borg

The walls in the lounge have holes like bullet holes,
but our walls do not have bullet holes.
Over the hallway, the ceiling is down as though bombed,
but our ceilings are not bombed.
The bathroom plumbing is exposed like a wound
in the body, but our body has not been wounded.
You are not in the house or garden,
but you are not dead and your photo on the mantelpiece
is not a memorial. The war does not shake the foundations
of the house, but the house is shaking.
We are not committing acts of which we are ashamed,
but we are ashamed. We have no simple enemies.
What is done in our name is not done in our name
but sullies us, is ours, is ours like our name.

Tom Chivers

SECURITY

Trick or Treaters are not all kids as
campers are not all happy and I wish
the banks would just start lending or
improve their customer service you know
I have to use a plastic keypad just to
check my balance which is invaluable
in the fight against fraud so when
you bowled towards me outside Bank
in the costume of the dead that is to say
masked and painted I had to ask the value
of that feint of pure hostility you are
clearly having fun which is a good thing
don't let me stop you

on my island none of this would be true

Mike Conley

These Three Young Ladies Have Come All The Way From Australia

says the compere. They wear
matching white vests and knickers
and they are jumping up and down on the spot,
holding hands. At first the room is silent enough
to hear the metronomic thumps, the soft kisses
of bare feet parting from beery stage floorboards
but after five minutes people are quietly
resuming conversation. After ten,
some get up to visit the bar or toilet
and after fifteen there is some heckling,
even booing. On twenty-four minutes,
the young lady in the middle stops
because her nose is bleeding.
Her colleagues on both sides continue to jump
and she grips their hands as the blood
pours around the corners of her wide smile,
down her chin, between her breasts.
On twenty-eight minutes
the noses of the other two young ladies
follow suit simultaneously and explosively,
splattering the tables at the front.
Out of breath, white vests stained red,
the young ladies bow at the waist. The blood
plumblines from their nostrils
and pools at their feet.
They exit stage right.

Sarah Corbett

BATH

Gutter as the cistern empties,
                parachute of steam un-rolling,
                     Esther in the half-light

                     candle flickers of hands,
          her shape cut on the wall.
She sings an unfamiliar song,

voice cracking for the reach
                of a word, then steep descent
                     of the melody. I dip in behind,

                     kiss her back, find the curve
          of her under the water in the slip
and ease of essence of roses

as she turns her mouth on mine,
                ash and acid of wine and cigarettes.
                Finish this, she says,

                     our bodies move as one joined
          snake enters and devours
to return whole from the throat,

the room given over,
                a smear on the wall the oil of her hair
                     scenting the room like a burn.

Damian Walford Davies

CORPUS

What can I say? I wasn't there:
neither ready to relieve him
of the transom's heft

at Via Dolorosa, Station number five;
nor standing with his mother
on the quarry's scree

to watch his wrists
spiked expertly
between electric nerve

and bone, and hear him
gurgle, drowning in the liquor
of his lungs. I could have tracked

the trail of blood
from here to where the last gob
hit the ground. The morning

had an air of perfect
commonplace. I howled,
so silently I know he heard.

Mark Doty

DEEP LANE

June 23rd, evening of the first fireflies,
we're walking in the cemetery down the road,
and I look up from my distracted study of whatever,

an unfocused gaze somewhere a few feet in front of my shoes,

and see that Ned has run on ahead
with the champagne plume of his tail held especially high,
his head erect,

which is often a sign that he has something he believes he is
    not allowed to have,

and in the gathering twilight (what is it that is gathered,
who is doing the harvesting?) I can make out that the long
    horizontal
between his lovely jaws is one of the four stakes planted on
    the slope

to indicate where the backhoe will dig a new grave.

Of course my impulse is to run after him, to replace the marker,
out of respect for the rule that we won't desecrate the tombs,
or at least for those who knew the woman whose name

inks a placard in the rectangle claimed by the four poles

of vanishing – three poles now – and how it's within their
  recollection,
their gathering, she'll live. Evening of memory. Spark-lamps
  in the grass.
I stand and watch him go in his wild figure eights,

I say, You run, darling, you tear up that hill.

Pescadero

The little goats like my mouth and fingers,

and one stands up against the wire fence, and taps on the
    fence-board
a hoof made blacker by the dirt of the field,

pushes her mouth forward to my mouth,
so that I can see the smallish squared seeds of her teeth, and
    the bristle-whiskers,

and then she kisses me, though I know it doesn't mean 'kiss',

then leans her head way back, arcing her spine, goat yoga,
all pleasure and greeting and then good-natured indifference:
    She loves me,

she likes me a lot, she takes interest in me, she doesn't know
    me at all
or need to, having thus acknowledged me. Though I am all
    happiness,

since I have been welcomed by the field's small envoy, and
    the splayed hoof,
fragrant with soil, has rested on the fence-board beside my
    hand.

Christy Ducker

Saint Cuthbert Banishes Demons from the Laser Clinic

He's sad to see my tattoo go
under the laser, blistering
from Lindisfarne knot to hot dough,
I got inked-up too young –
too full of hell, I say to him
and he smiles his hermit crab smile,
suggests I think of the Book
his acolyte wrote on skin
with soot and gold, how it reconciles
gannets, cats and dogs as word
of love, how every page is flawed
on purpose, saying to people
perfection makes us much too proud –
wear your mistakes like gospel.

Dan Duggan

DRESSMAKING

They laid both wrists face up like
dead fish, and the hour glass over to
the left. A cold bar of sterile

light illuminating the flesh like
sun through a stained glass window.

I watched one stitch, the other follow,
like a corset being tied for a staid evening
of tiresome conversation, a radio, whale

bones, the satin disappearing under caution,
then the neat gasp of satisfaction,
and the finished garment.
It must have been

early morning when they took me to bed…

Inua Ellams

SHAME IS THE CAPE I WEAR.

On the first day of holidays, my mother leaves a dark blue
wrapper on her bed, her polished boots in one corner and
in no time, I assemble a superhero costume to defend our
house against the plague of lizards: their spindly children,

tongues flicking, nodding under afternoon heat – they are
a reptilian evil. Every hero needs a nemesis. This cotton
cape casts me as Naija's Superman and they threaten life
in the Lagos metropolis. No matter the property you buy,

how tight-shut the gutters, how climb-proof the walls, also
how sharp their crown of barbwires, lizards come. Father,
who insists a clean well-swept backyard helps, is away and
the long-tailed legions are confidently swarming all about

the place, across air vents, up the garden's wire mesh too
thin to survive their claws. Anyway, I'm hovering by that
mesh, a rubber band stretched between my fingers, cape
flowing and a quiver of toothpick-thick bristles, one curled

against the taut elastic. I catch a lizard's beady steady eyes,
take aim, fire, and watch the bristle break through its back,
first piercing its soft stomach and my aim just gets better.
An hour, and there are bodies piled. Above, a commotion of

flies, excitable over the stiffening flesh and blood and I have
watched my shadow lengthen to cover the grey and redhead
corpses, the backyard a silent killing field, and I could almost
feel that flowing cape deflate. Sometimes I think that little

boy in his mother's work boots has followed me my whole life through. There he is when I'm laughing at a party and find a crimson drink spilled across the clean carpet or when I look in a mirror to see what the years have done to me or when

I flick through news channels and catch a war time president speak of quick victories, of collateral damage and first class weapons, the locals broken behind soldiers and men in tweed who will fabricate stories of jubilant cheers and fist pumps

and shame is the cape I wear that day, shame and that little boy, that shadow, is there his head hanging down as it did then, his hands shaking.

Steve Ely

The Battle of Brunanburgh: II

On Weondune, holy hill, grass-slope greased with
   guts, I creep with purse-nets, metal detector,
   the Observer's Book of Bird's Eggs. I peg and
   dig and delve.

Whose is this land? The grass grows brittle on
   leaching bones of Scots; golf club
   groundsmen weed and spray; farmers lurk,
   keepers oil their shotguns.

With needle and cotton, I converted my parka to a
   coat of many pockets; catchstitch,
   backstitch, my *opus anglicanum*. On the
   right-of-way by STRICTLY PRIVATE, I slip
   away quickly, ignoring shouts and raking
   torchbeams. Partridge-pearled, furred with
   coneys, lining full of coin: Æthelstan, *Rex
   totius Britanniae.*

Elaine Feinstein

Life Class: A Sketch

In Paris, perhaps. On wet cobbles,
walking alone at night, fragile
and wispily dressed, Jean Rhys,
without a *sou*, past streets
of lit cafés to a meeting place.

Cold to the bone, she has it all planned:
when they go home, she'll fall
at his knees, gaze up like a child,
and make him understand
he cannot abandon her,

lost in a strange land.
His grey eyes are indifferent as
the North Sea to her need –
if she tries to plead
her words will drown.

So she smiles instead.
That's how she'll cope with crooks
and pick-ups, drink and veronal
in those grim boarding houses
that now stretch ahead.

Over and over she will write the story
of frail girls and the unkindness of men,
speaking in the voice of her cool notebooks,
until one day a frightened Creole self
climbs down from the attic of memory

in the shape of the first Mrs Rochester,
betrayed, barefoot, imprisoned
in an England of snow and roses,
constrained in Thornfield Hall, a dangerous
ghost – that apparition brings success.

Jean entertains in a Knightsbridge hotel,
elegant in her seventies to meet her fame,
with eyes like dark blue pools:
'Too late,' she says, 'Too late', without irony,
as her looks fade – into a ninth decade.

Annie Freud

The Jeweller

This is a speaking piece.
It suits you to perfection. It is yours already.
You think I say that because of your dark colouring?
No, it is more than that. It is your nature.
It knows you better than you know yourself.
Jewels have a language of their own
and every piece has something particular to say
that only the giver and receiver hear:
father to daughter,
sister to sister,
son to mother,
master to servant,
husband to wife,
lover to lover.
The intention is always love,
different kinds of never-ending love.
Those who come after can only imagine.

And these, you want to know are they real diamonds?
Are not my Oms, my Buddhas and mudras, my Vishnus, Ganeshas,
pashminas, my lingams and yonis and sandalwood backscratchers, real?
They are all versions and facsimiles.

These stones are zircon, Madam,
but only if you look very closely would you know,
and they are pure, purer even than diamonds.

Alan Gillis

You must have seen those Rent Street potheads,
their skin all sweating processed chicken meat:
knives taped to their thighs, blood-red dots for eyes,
stolen shoes like rocketblasters on their feet?

As sure as rainfall, they're at the entrance to the mall,
tattooed necks livid with love bites.
Hooked to mobile phones, they know your way home
and they wait for you in alleyways at night.

They spit on the bus, their fingers are warty,
they set fire to schools, sniff WD40,
they climb any fence, they climb any roof,
they jump on your bonnet and smash your sunroof,

they'll squeeze through your window and creep up your stairs,
they'll leave your comb crawling with their pubic hairs,
they'll crowbar your gold teeth right out of your head,
they excrete on the street, and they don't go to bed.

John Glenday

"Gignit et Oceanus margarita, sed subfusca ac liventia…"
                                        (Tacitus Agricola 1:12)

British pearls are exceptionally poor.
They can be gathered up by the handful wherever
surf breaks, but you'll find no colour, no vitality, no lustre
to them – every last one stained the roughshod grey
of their drab and miserable weather.

Imagine all the rains of this island held
in one sad, small, turbulent world.
I can hear them falling as I write. British pearls
are commonplace and waterish and dull,
but their women wear them as if winter were a jewel.

Philip Gross

THE PLAYERS

Somewhere in a square in the old world, by the Hotel Princip,
    by the Palace of Justice, somewhere in a park
        of clean gravel and poodle-cut trees

beside cobblestones seamed with tramlines, somewhere near
    a kiosk café whose waiter, in stubble and butcher-
        striped apron will fail to appear,

sometimes for days, at three wrought iron tables, bearing
    coffees concentrated to a fierce point, a black
        hole – one sip will suck you in,

turned to sparkling stone… Somewhere like this they sit, two
    old men, each one older than the other.
        Bending forward, they sit at a pace

from which the three-lane traffic is a shimmery smear,
    a mirage, oil on water, and the pieces
        themselves seem a fidget,

a jitter of cause and effect which leaves no choice but,
    now and then, to lift a hand… a moment's
        late appraisal, as the world

turns one more orbit. One
                moves. Looks up. The other
    nods. I've seen them at the black and white
        marble table with the raised squares

in the Garden for the Blind, a table like a plinth
    on which they are building ice sculptures
        of certain uncertainties, and

it is beautiful, very, they might say. If ever they spoke.
    (Kibbitzers do the chatter for them.) They
        live, if indeed they do,

in twenty worlds at once, all intercutting: *if, and if*
    not, then, and if then, not… Every
        thirty years or so, a bang:

slammed door or backfire of exhaust, and now and then
    a handgun. All the combinations shatter
        into flight, up

over rooftops, dewlapped gables, weather vanes
    to reform, circle, circle, homing
        on wherever we may be.

Marilyn Hacker

Pantoum in Wartime

In memory of Adrienne Rich

Were the mountain women sold as slaves
in the city my friend has not written from for two weeks?
One of the Just has given back his medal.
I wake up four times in the night soaked with sweat.

In the city my friend has not written from, for two weeks
there was almost enough electricity.
I wake up four times in the night soaked with sweat
and change my shirt and go to sleep again.

There was almost enough electricity
to heat water, make tea, bathe, write e-mails
and change her shirt and go to sleep again.
Her mother has gallstones. Her sister mourns.

Heat water, make tea, bathe, write e-mails
to Mosul, New York, London, Beirut.
Her sister mourns a teenaged son who died
in a stupid household accident.

To Mosul, Havana, London, Beirut,
I change the greeting, change the alphabet.
War like a stupid household accident
changes the optics of a scene forever.

I change the greeting, change the alphabet:
Hola, morning of light, ya compañera.
Change the optics of a scene forever
present, and always altogether elsewhere.

Morning of roses, kiss you, hasta luego
to all our adolescent revolutions,
present and always altogether elsewhere.
It seemed as if something would change for good tomorrow.

All our adolescent revolutions
gone gray, drink exiles' coffee, if they're lucky.
It seemed as if something would change for good tomorrow.
She was our conscience and she died too early.

The gray exiles drink coffee, if they're lucky.
Gaza's survivors sift through weeping rubble.
She was our conscience, but she died too early,
after she spoke of more than one disaster.

Cursing, weeping, survivors sift through rubble.
One of the Just has given back his medal,
after he spoke of more than one disaster.
How can we sing our songs if we are slaves?

Selima Hill

C

When Agatha arranges her unicorns
up and down the carpet in the dark,
somebody tells her she's an idiot –
but what she needs is a little hairdryer.

MY FATHER AS A LORRY

If a large refrigerated lorry
were made of sunshine, all my little friends

would marvel at it as they would at him
if my father were to speak to them.

Jane Hirshfield

My Life Was the Size of My Life

My life was the size of my life.
Its rooms were room-sized,
its soul was the size of a soul.
In its background, mitochondria hummed,
above it sun, clouds, snow,
the transit of stars and planets.
It rode elevators, bullet trains,
various airplanes, a donkey.
It wore socks, shirts, its own ears and nose.
It ate, it slept, it opened
and closed its hands, its windows.
Others, I know, had lives larger.
Others, I know, had lives shorter.
The depth of lives, too, is different.
There were times my life and I made jokes together.
There were times we made bread.
Once, I grew moody and distant.
I told my life I would like some time,
I would like to try seeing others.
In a week, my empty suitcase and I returned.
I was hungry, then, and my life,
my life, too, was hungry, we could not keep
our hands off   our clothes on
our tongues from

Rosalind Hudis

Salvage

I dreamed I was in water beyond a vessel
where babies were being born. It was all
black gloss in motion, liquid molasses.
Lights pierced and spasmed white
or electric blue. There was the sense
of a port on standby, ship horns, signals
meant and broken, voices became a low
concussion, peaked and fell and always
if I tried to board, I was waved away.

And I understood that we were at a border
where there was no transmission and no
codes to permit us. I woke, breathed clear
the room we had arrived in, still bare
dawn emptying its sediment, becoming
yellow, alive with pigeon calls,
sky half way risen, pushing
its holy crust. My newborn child there
like something salvaged, a tiny figurine,

wheat skinned, which I knew to be a passing
jaundice and her sloped eyes the unpassing
grain of her life. For now, all hours were tidal
cooled, re-heated. A mid-wife brought us tulips.
Refilled my cup. It seemed enough
– to moor ourselves in ebb
in surge, not in the babel of birds, engines,
voices. I watched the sunlight prove
door, ceiling, window, name-tag, cradle, breath.

Peter Hughes

19 / 223

Qual donna attende a gloriosa fama

the ads & features in the magazines
can be a bit misleading when it comes
to becoming more attractive & wise
slimming & swimming & staying the same

relationships between self-esteem &
the hair-do branded jumper numbered pew
sponsorship of glazed cyclists new string
quartets & party donations stop here

her subtle use of pauses brings to mind
Miles Davis & those tunes that run alongside
other people's language at the bar

it's hard to say how much she learned & how
much she was born with but she's borne it well
towards that bourn from which no traveller

Ishion Hutchinson

MR. KILLDEER'S COLD COMFORT

All through January's silence,
my neighbour, Mr. Killdeer,

crosses with peaches and jalapeños
to thaw the hiatus in my ivy

and holly home, a candle
lit at dusk to shadows scrutinizing

from corners, stretching to touch
our low voices on the porch.

Mr. Killdeer, forensic, slices
a peach, pits a pepper, 'My wife Darla

is a straight shot, great with the M1911...'
and so forth, guttering, until,

heliotropic, green-eyed gristles
stare up from the plate. I raise one

and bite into bone cold air.
His eyes watered, mine for the basalt,

sun-incubating-frosted streets,
the cathedral bells' quarterly

obit phlegm up in my ears.
I do not sleep; I kneel nights

in the book barracks, hoarding
a caravel to return to my birth

sea, back to the tuning fork peninsula,
an opened valve contradiction

in the town square, the roadside
cane flags glinting through marl

and dust out at Folly Oval,
the cemetery tumbling down

to the barley cricket pitch.
My brain edges: In this America,

this wilderness…too long dumb,
Mr. Killdeer folds his Swiss,

departs into the snow.
I rise to reenter the Arctic

silhouette, certain it is no longer
a miracle to stand on water.

Clive James

WINTER PLUMS

Two winter plum trees grow beside my door.
Throughout the cold months they had little pink
Flowers all over them as if they wore
Nightdresses, and their branches, black as ink
By sunset, looked as if a Japanese
Painter, while painting air, had painted these

Two winter plum trees. Summer now at last
Has warmed their leaves and all the blooms are gone.
A year that I might not have had has passed.
Bare branches are my signal to go on,
But soon the brave flowers of the winter plums
Will flare again, and I must take what comes:

Two winter plum trees that will outlive me.
Thriving with colour even in the snow,
They'll snatch a triumph from adversity.
All right for them, but can the same be so
For someone who, seeing their buds remade
From nothing, will be less pleased than afraid?

Sarah James

Lies shriek loudest at night,
when Carl sighs   beside me.

3am. Something battles
against the water pipes.

The chimney coughs.
Our fridge's purr turns

to fierce roar. Claws scrape
on near bricks, the bushes snarl.

Then a car door slams –
in a stifled metal kiss.

The walls' muffled thuds,
shuffling floorboard creakings

and the wind in the rafters
all hiss 'We know!'

Martha Kapos

She Dressed Him Entirely

Taking it down from the hook
with panoramic holes for his head and arms
she dressed him entirely

in the present moment, the confirming
yes to everything he said
tucking him up in bed, smoothing

the sheets, laying out the views
from the window: all the shapes
she made of the blue-green

grapevine hung over the garage
the sumac with its many-budded spikes
placed on the curving lawn

so that he proceeded among them
into the deep garden where trees
displayed their new collections of leaves

each waving a long stem towards him
holding a lozenge of green light
as if they were extensions of his own eye

and the sky stood open in motionless
pieces of shining the size of a diamond.
Her face in its largeness swam

on a repeating wave of arrival
coming as it did from a place
where the sun sat on his bed as if

it would never move, never go into eclipse
behind the sliding shadow of a door
or ever give up its shape and grow thin.

Mimi Khalvati

Knifefish

Lit, lit, lit, lit are the estates at dawn:
honeycomb stairwells, corridors, landing lights,

flare paths for passengers flying home.
Three jets like electric fish streak the sky with rose.

Black ghost, ghost knifefish, how many days
since you went abroad, lurking in your murky pools,

locating dawn by sonar, by electric fields alone?
To image your world in darkness – driftwood

casting distortion shadows – no matter how weak
your receptor organ, faint its discharge, barely a volt,

through tail-bend, waveform, you fire, you feel,
sensing lightning, earthquake, your own kind

turning their dimmer switch up and down,
for this is how you talk. Old Aba Aba, grandpa,

with your one room lit at a time, feeling for walls,
navigating as surely as in the brightest, highest dawn!

Angels

Updraughts lift sounds of language imperceptibly, even
the silent language of Lula as she hobbles up the steps.

Dogs Lula doesn't know bark along the terraces, cockerels,
though it isn't dawn, crow anyway. It could be any village

anywhere in the world, everything in decay. But things
retain their scent – the rubbed tomato leaf – and sound

– the bamboo river – and as if heard behind closed doors,
the angels: angel of September, of the fallen fig and dapple;

angel of perspective that staggers the terraces upward,
white steps downward; angels of the sister mountains –

the first, the second, the third. And the angels, cowled,
circle us like lepers on the hills, they unveil themselves.

And I love my angels not as they were in childhood,
angel of the crab-apple and chine, of calico and sandal,

but as they are: leprous and discharged, violent and betrayed.
Angel of the soft wind that blows across my breasts.

Frances Leviston

Parma Violet

Egyptian sofas, old anaglypta,
the drop-leaf table where the pine tree posed
every mild December,
on its pedestal the dodo, crackle-glazed,
and hung above the hearth and the dormant fire
a painting I supposed

must be a distant cousin, or a great grandmother,
but was neither of those –
only a junk-shop likeness of a stranger,
all tarnished oils and shadows,
that when my friends visited made them shudder
in the cruel, exaggerated manner of girls.

A Gothic effect, the narrow shoulder
turned aside, the plain, black, high-necked blouse;
governess, or dowager,
she looked severe to them. I found her serious,
and since there was no other
for her I invented any history that pleased:

hair powder, mystic wills, Parma
violets dry on the tongue, big lozenges loose
in iconic tins, and the sampler's
motto: *Family is Furniture* – charge to which I rose
in spite of myself, like a hair in thunder –
if I wasn't hers, then whose?

Midsummer Loop

now in the stillness, the two still hours
between this meeting and that,
hours of silence in which the angel of conversation deserts us
to beat her wings above another gathering,
another long room, magnificent table and solemn pronouncement
made to the detriment of everybody else
and the glorification of the subject,
now we are abandoned to our own resources
on this one original summer's day
and two hours fill like stones with the heat of the afternoon,
two flat stones placed on the stomach to steady
the heartbeat and the breathing,
a number of rabbits
emerge from their secret holes hidden about campus,
hidden but not undiscoverable holes
down in the beginnings of dry holly-bushes out of season
and the naked wooden roots of rhododendrons
from which the rabbits hop forward one hop at a time, one a minute,
a hundred little clepsydras
all set to different schedules, forward
on to the grass, where they balance, weightless as empty pelts
on the points of the blades, like martial artists
who lie unharmed on beds of nails
conducting their spiritual business, with two hot stones
weighing down their bodies, lightly, painlessly,
rabbits fanning out
across the sweeps of grass that sustain them,
across the blades that do not bend beneath them,
where they eat with endless hunger and fanatical devotion,
clipping flat the sharp tips
precisely with ordinary, curved, discoloured teeth
again and again, masticating the strands
as they cross and re-cross the blocks of dark gold sun
laid across the lawns like golden doors
through which we cannot pass, through which they pass unharmed,

both ears laid flat like banked canoes
and their great hind legs gentle and relaxed,
white scuts bobbing
quietly across the campus, which is also their campus,
attached as rabbits are attached to their shadows
to a vast university invisible underground, the one ours mirrors,
intricate halls of residence and studios
round which the rabbits conduct themselves
in absolute darkness, by touch and smell alone, the wordless
sensitivities of their whiskers
brushing the walls and other warm bodies
or thrilling to an offensive discharge of fear in the air
undetectable to the human
who feels so pleased to have spotted
two rabbit-holes, there, at the foot of that blossoming tree,
now in the stillness, the two still hours
between this meeting and that

John McAuliffe

SHED

for Peter Fallon

I bought the shed, for a song, off a neighbour
who'd stopped using it after he paved the garden.
He'd inherited it or got it somewhere he couldn't remember,
not that I gave a second thought to its origin.

It was heavier than it looked so he helped take the roof to pieces.
After an hour prying out each crooked tack
we levered off its grey-green sandpaper stiffness
and rested it, on the drive, like a book stranded on its back.

The neighbour, looking at his watch, said, 'Let's push',
and the four walls and floor did move – a little.
In front of the garage, sweating, feeling each
ounce of the previous night, we saw too late

it was too big to go through. We counted the nails but couldn't:
they were like stars, more the more we looked. 'Heave it over,'
over the garage and down, he joked,
the garden path to its resting place under the magnolia.

No joke: we made a ramp of the ladder and inched
this half-tonne pine crate up and out of the road.
The scraped-flat garage roof pitched
under our careful feet. Two euphoric beers later, after we'd lowered

it into place, we agreed on twenty quid. Every so often
he still calls in: today he's selling up and getting out.
He asks about the shed. I say it's fine, so half hidden
by April gusts of leaf and petal he can hardly see it,

as we look, out the window, at where it leans
against the fence, painted green, the unlocked door
opening on the lawnmower and half-full cans
of paint and petrol, pure potential, evaporating into the air.

But work makes work: paving the lot, he volunteers, makes
    more sense.
I'm offering him a cup of tea
when, before he can collect himself, he starts to resent
the twenty quid and leaving the shed behind: 'It was,' he says,
    'almost free.'

Chris McCabe

A New Way to Pay Old Debts

Spoken by Alworth in rage against Overreach, an aspiring landowner. Alworth has fallen in love with Overreach's daugher Margaret, although Overreach is determined for his daughter to marry the noble Lord Lovell. We are here, Drury Lane, 1621.

Toenails blàck in the petty càsh   burnt pennies
        You cormorant   You catspaw   You cruel
extórtioner   beer & debt gnaw my endórphins
        You brach   You dogbolt   You hellhound
        beats & kicks him ThIS IS THe ANNiversArY
of SEL1INg YoUR SoUL TO H+t INsURAncE ApR
549%   This credit card you don't want has your
name on it   it can be couriered by Three Creditors
        You lean skull   You privy creature   You
sláve to meat   Fill this glass with whíte froth &
watch me knock it off   You buyer   You drudge
        You ditch to what's inside   Enter "human skulls in
the Thames"   ERROR 404   You hedge-funders to
our best Players   You bond-slave   You cur

You son of incest   You cherrylipped mannequin of
blàck plots   After The George & the youth you saw
in my face   outside the Barclays where I signed my
name like a hair in whítebroth   *buttermilk cheeks*
        where I knew, at the Strand, there was no money
in poetry   but heard   in the truth of gráves
after   drinkings,   when   you   lodg'd upon the Bankside
there   is   NEVER   any   poetry   in   càsh

Kate Miller

At the Root of the Wind is Strife   *according to Empedocles*

after dark

sevenish, December, when a reveller on the South Bank lifts a bag,
                    opens it, out sneaks – freed

from the mythic bag of winds – a hungry gust with a taste for plastic
                    wrap and smeared empties

after weeks of diet: crazy for a lick at cans lodged in the crook
                    of evergreens. Enter, inebriated

wind round midnight, now to leap and beat as waves do, reaching
                    house fronts, occasionally gale

force, upstart alarms and make the sirens weep.

daylight

                    Twelve hours on, the morning
mind's so tuned to monochrome it dwells on carcrash,

                    intimations of fatality.
A garden's unnerved, pinched beneath the flight path;

                    if roses could despair,
they'd sink this low, ashen, winter-worsened.

                    Two police whichwaydegoes
increase in whush, very rapid and another hornlike,

                    dooda dooda, as it spins,
whirling Catherine wheel of earsplit, banshee band.

daylong

Air over London is a mountain
tunnelled through with din, draughts down every stack and chimney,

mineshafts,
squeal, clank, crashed gears, thumped drums. Workers wield a thousand

picks and hammers,
tocktock, gamelan tingtang, staccato clock tick, clock on, clock off,

ambulances' rising whistles
ripple east flingflingaling to new emergency quick birth attack or fire

accelerating. Bully wind
                    and bully's patter runs to bellow, bluster.

dark again

Hanged woman on the street, neck noosed by her long hair,
                    man with pent-up pitbull

shrinks from the rain's harangue, the quaking glass in walls.
                    Bus tides suck and swirl

delivering crocodiles in gutters. Thunder in gouts, all hail
                    on windscreens, buckshot

diamonds pock and tag, the final push at nineteenhundred.
                    Landing craft and minicabs

attend the mess, the muddled men, the downed, drowned-out,
                    sound-sickened in the day-long skirmish.

Les Murray

HIGH RISE

Fawn high rise of Beijing
with wristwatch-shaped
air conditioners on each window

and burglar bars to the tenth
level in each new city,
white-belted cylinders of dwelling

around every Hong Kong bay –
Latest theory is, the billions
will slow their overbreeding

only when consuming in the sky.
Balconious kung fu of Shanghai.
A nineteenth floor lover

heroic among consumer goods
slips off the heights of desire
down the going-home high wire –

above all the only children.

Togara Muzanenhamo

ALDERFLIES

Naked and afraid, the girl doubled up with a shrill
that filled the rear-view, the red sun thick off her hair,
her lips peeled back over teeth clenched on tails of air
shredded thin by speed. A rush of rich carmine silt ran
swollen under the bridge, the dry knock of the wheel
pitching the battered Hilux over the ungraded road.
Again her face resurfaced, alone in the mirror, the strain
of the breech birth tightening her breath, the road
rolling stoically to its cruel end where a dirt-strip took
us up to a quiet clinic set at the foot of the mountain.
There, blood and limb turned cold between her thighs.
The drive back home was all silver light and tussock
grass fields, low heavy gears moaning to the turn-off –
the road speckled black, the river's bruised serigraph
woven wet with the brisk evening flight of alderflies.

Sean O'Brien

AUDIOLOGY

I hear an elevator sweating in New Orleans,
Water folding black on black in tanks deep under Carthage,
Unfracked oil in Lancashire
And what you're thinking. It's the truth –
There goes your silent count to ten, the held breath
Of forbearance, all the language not yet spoken
Or unspeakable, the dark side of the page.
But this is not about you. I can hear
The sea drawn back from Honshu,
Hookers in the holding pen, and logorrhoea
In the dreaded Quiet Coach,
The firestorm of random signs
On market indices, the bull, the bear,
The sound of one hand clapping and the failure of the rains,
The crackle of the dried-out stars,
Stars being born, anomalies and either/or,
The soundtrack of creation in an unrecorded vowel,
The latest that might be the last, the leading edge
Of all that is the case or is not there.
'The contradictions cover such a range.'
And I'm told that soon it will be easier
To balance out the love-cry and the howl,
To wear an aid and act my age, to hear the world
Behind this world and not to crave amnesia.

Ruth Padel

EMERALD

Below is the same as above, says the Emerald Tablet
Jung saw in a dream. You've passed Security,
you're entering the mine. You were looking for love:
try the mysteries of earth. Put on the waterproof,
hard hat, rubber boots and gloves. You found it
in the Vedas: *Emeralds bring luck.*

You're winched into the dark on a platform-cage
through a rushing flood. Can you trust the chains?
The water's warm, the motor rattles, the temperature
is hot enough to suffocate, stop Orpheus in his song.
Forty metres. Forty more. At the bottom,
a sauna labyrinth of carbon, formed

by the tectonic shunt that made the Andes.
Torchlight. Blackened faces. They don't get salaries,
they're paid for what they find. Do you, the adept
of "Theatrum Chemicum", desire the formula,
the liquid and gas chromium and vanadium
crystallised to hexagon in boiling brine?

You slosh, crouching, through water.
A hundred claw-points tease the roof,
the pitch-black honeycomb
of tunnels haunted by a glint-fire ghost
of absinthe, Nefertiti, Melusine.
The call comes *Here!* and everyone stampedes.

A thousand jackhammers, ten thousand ricochets
and a raw rock-face brocade of dazzle-green.
Any pick-swing could make your fortune.
You're surrounded, oxygen levels plummet
and you don't care for this is the myth
of all myths. Jackpot. The suddenly answered prayer.

Overhead, slow sunrise stipples emerald slopes
of cloud forest and sugar cane, to rose.
Children trawl abandoned shafts. Women search
breast-deep in the river for a glimpse of the Enchanter.
Streaked faces, wild eyes in a panda blur –
that's all of us in our anonymities and hope.

Below is the same as above. Emerald is wire
fencing, a guard with pump-action shotgun,
the paramilitaries of Victor Carranza, cartel king,
and the black mud dance of chaos. Children know
you reach the Emerald City only on ruby slippers.
Emerald is blood. But somehow you make it back

to the market-place. La Candelaria looks
like any square: small lunch-bars and glum
traffic. The emeralds are invisible, carried in twists
of paper to open air. The only light dealers trust
to check for flux-grown polymers, synthetic glass
from labs in California, is the Incas' naked sun.

Emerald is heart of alchemy. Ferny bubbles,
mystical imperfections, flaws that make each stone
unique, trapped in mineral as it forms
like fantasies embedded in the soul.
Emerald is spring, translating underworld
to stony idioms of the brain,

a kingfisher reflected in the secret bowl
of ocean. Verdant but easily chipped,
healing but poison, colour of Venus, birthstone of May,
but also the green-eyed monster. Double-edged.
Watch a dealer hold new facets to the sky. It's a risk,
renewing dreams. It's putting yourself through hell

like Orpheus, not knowing what you'll lose.
In one small blazing stone – as green as grass,
as Acamar or Rastaban, the brightest stars –
you face what transformation means. Ask
the *commissionista*. This is the life
you'll pay for. Open his paper. Choose.

Don Paterson

MERCIES

She might have had months left of her dog-years,
but to be who? She'd grown light as a nest
and spent the whole day under her long ears
listening to the bad radio in her breast.
On the steel bench, knowing what was taking shape
she tried and tried to stand, as if to sign
that she was still of use, and should escape
our selection. So I turned her face to mine,
and seeing only love there – which, for all
the wolf in her, she knew as well as we did –
she lay back down and let the needle enter.
And love was surely what her eyes conceded
as her stare grew hard, and one bright aerial
quit making its report back to the centre.

A Threshold

Where have you gone, my little saving grace?
Iona or Iola of the laugh
like falling silver… Now nothing's in its place,
and all's as light and cold as that blue scarf
I lost or left without, or I don't own.
Everything shames me. Every card declined.
You slid between the stalls and you were gone
though I scoured the field for hours, hoping to find
you sat with 'the silent children of the fair'
or some such nonsense, though I always knew
you'd taken another hand, the way kids do,
not looking up. This place again. It's where
I wake up and recall I have no daughter
or fall asleep and dream I have no daughter.

Rebecca Perry

SOUP SISTER

And, of course,
it bothers me greatly that I can't know
the quality of the light where you are.
How your each day pans out,
how the breeze lifts the dry leaves from the street
or how the street pulls away from the rain.

Last week I passed a tree
that was exactly you in tree form,
with a kind look and tiny sub-branches
like your delicate wrists.

Six years ago we were lying
in a dark front room on perpendicular sofas,
so hungover that our skin hurt to touch.
How did we always manage
to be heartbroken at the same time?

I could chop, de-seed and roast
a butternut squash for dinner
in the time it took you to shower.

Steam curtained the windows, whiting out
the rain, which hit the house sideways.
One of us, though I forget who, said
do you think women are treated like bowls
waiting to be filled with soup?
And the other one said, of course.

Now the world is too big,
and it's sinking and rising
and stretching out its back bones.

The rivers are too wild,
the mountains are so so old
and it's all laid out arrogantly between us.

My friend, how long do you stand
staring at the socks in your drawer
lined up neat as buns in a bakery,
losing track of time and your place in the world,
in the (custardy light of a) morning?

Katrina Porteous

COBLE COUNTING SONG

Eight boats moored in Beadlin Hyeven.
Woman looks oot an' she sees just seven.

A stoene for the drooned in Beadlin chorchyard:
Sometimes a woman can see ower-much, lad.

A poond a foot, a poond a foot,
A poond a foot a cowble cost.

BK 6 was a Boulmer cowble,
Changed hor name for' the *Mary Twizell*:

Fowerteen drooned in a blinnd snaa' flurry.
Hoo much grief can a cowble carry?

A poond a foot, a poond a foot.

Five was the cowbles sailed for' Beadlin
Roond t' the Clyde t' fish for harrin';

Forth an' Clyde was the gates a heaven,
Hell was the timm'ers an' a sail t' sleep in.

A poond a foot, a poond a foot.

Fower was the last crew ontae Longstone
Night a the Blizzard i' the line-time. Someone

Spied 'em driftin' ower the Kni'stone;
That much ice that he scarcely knew them.

A poond a foot, a poond a foot.

Three was the crew a the boat *Provider* –
Sank an' drooned steamin' hyem t' Craster;

Ran away on a sooth-east lipper,
Broadside ontae the sea, booled ower.

Cowble's a grand boat heed t' weather;
Runnin' afore it – divvin't bother.

A poond a foot, a poond a foot.

Tew was the sea-byeuts yen man's widder
Hid in a cupboard wi' the hard, black sorrer

Shut at the bottom of hor throat forivvor.
Tew is a number bad t' shatter.

A poond a foot, a poond a foot.

Yen was a skipper from the Heedlan' Fish Quay,
May God rest him and bless his family.

A cowble was nivvor a boat for yen.
Yen is a number that ends in naen.

Tell me what, noo tell me what,
Aye, tell me what a cowble cost.

All the incidents referred to in this poem are true. A memorial stone in
Beadnell churchyard records the loss of four members of the Fawcus
family, drowned within sight of home, on 31 January 1885. The *Mary
Twizell* was one of four cobles lost from Blyth and Newbiggin with
fourteen lives in a snowstorm on 18 March 1915. The Blizzard referred to
in stanza seven took place on 6 February 1895: a Seahouses coble was lost
with two lives and many Seahouses and Beadnell fishermen took shelter
on the Farne Islands. The *Provider* was lost from Craster on 10 February
1928 with three lives. Hartlepool fisherman Edward Bissell was lost from
his coble *Bonny Lass* on 18 January 2006. 'A poond a foot' was said to be
what it cost to build a coble in the late 19th century.

Wendy Pratt

Amazing Grace

Here is the divide: on the one side,
the pregnant wife, on the other,
the grieving mother. And in between:
a father; a husband, a man in a vacuum
as the surgeons run past. After the sudden
hydraulic drop of the time of death being called,
the woman will emerge; a sleeping Cleopatra
on a white barge.

That little thing they lost in the rush
between pregnancy and birth is a sink hole
beneath them; sudden and inexplicable.
And don't they look uncomfortable
for the photos; no natural smiles, their heads
are flicking back and forth, knowing that these
are the only images they'll have, and really,
they should look happy for eternity, rather
than in-the-moment-grief stricken.

Like shuffling cards, those emotions. Then here,
at three AM, as the fan glides round again
and halogen anoints her husband, wrapped
as he is on that camp bed, she lays on her side
staring at the puddle of lamp light that illuminates
her daughter, and wonders how she can feel so lost,
but yet so found.

Padraig Regan

APPLES, CHERRIES, APRICOTS & OTHER FRUITS IN A BASKET, WITH
PEARS, PLUMS, ROBINS, A WOODPECKER, A PARROT, & A MONKEY
EATING NUTS ON A TABLE

after Clara Peeters

I can't stay angry at my little capuchin even though I was looking
    forward to those walnuts
which he holds in his wonderfully long fingers like an anatomist
    giving a lecture on the brain,
before nibbling at the edges as if he was some sort of metaphor
    for some sort of neurological disease.

I know that I cannot trust my little capuchin around fresh fruit:
    what he doesn't eat he smears on the walls
in a fragrant impasto. At first I thought to indulge these creations
    but the black crusts of flies (his only patrons)
were more than I could tolerate. I tried to make him stop & he
    crushed a nectarine into my face.

Whenever my little capuchin looks up at me with those big,
    paperweight eyes, I find reserves
of forgiveness that I never knew existed; suddenly I don't mind so
    much about the broken plates, the shredded
tapestries, the piss-stains on the sofa, the nutty grenades of shit
    he throws to welcome visitors.

He knows that quivering his little capuchin chin & shaking his
    tail is enough to make me turn the other
cheek to the bodies of robins, woodpeckers, parrots, & other
    birds which are littered around his haunches
like the shells of those walnuts which he holds in his wonderfully
    long fingers like a puppeteer.

Christopher Reid

The Cyclists

The cyclists took the corner
in italics. An entire paragraph.
We drew in and let them hurtle by.
Lean, fixed on speed,
they paid no attention to us.
They were a flashed warrant,
an illegible screed
of backs uniformly cursive
and curlicued handlebars.
Or a thigh-powered,
air-slicing machine
for clearing the roads of France.
Or the corps de ballet
in its celebrated showstopper,
Get Out of Our Way!
Or – in helmets, goggles
and gaudy lycra –
a new species of insect,
related to the grasshopper
and, through some fluke of evolution,
blessed with wheels.
Windows down, we felt their breeze.
But they paid no attention to us.
Sly, weekend lovers, we were less
than a footnote. The text
had only itself to please.

Sam Riviere

Let us draw near to Russia.
Let us go right into the presence of film criticism.
Let us celebrate music since 2002.
Let us give out pies and eat corn dogs.

Jump to The Sound of Young America
with its undercurrents of guilty conscience.
We have been sprinkled with sauce by radio hosts,
not with the old blood,

nor with the speech espoused to make us clean,
not old D. H. Lawrence.
But even here we suspected as much.
It's now (a satire).

Therefore keep the network peace.
Therefore label the location,
with a heart in full idea,
with hearts fully defined in American English.

Greta Stoddart

LIFEGUARD

Of course I know he meant nothing to me
alive, why would he, a part-time lifeguard
at the local pool I'd only ever glimpse
slumped in a plastic chair or standing deep
in a cupboard leaning his chin on a mop.
The only thing that passed between us
was a look – almost cold from us both –
when I asked him for armbands, the hard kind.
He handed them to me as if I wasn't there.
The day he died I drove past Skindeep
and saw him outside on the pavement, smoking,
squinting in the late afternoon sun,
his shaved head, his stumpy legs.
Yes, I remember thinking, that fits, that crew –
pierced, tattooed, the hair (too much or none), the bikes.
And glancing in the rear view mirror I saw
the line of his head almost golden in the dust.
A few hours later I walked into the pool foyer
and there, to one side – a sheaf of lilies
in a mop-bucket and a small table
where a few sweaty carnations were scattered
around three photos in a plastic sleeve:
one of him looking very small on his bike;
another he must've taken himself, it had that
mild looming look of a fish swimming up
to its own reflection; and one of him
hunched over a naked back, needle in hand,
with such a look of care and concentration
I almost felt his breath on the back of my neck.
People were walking past and buying tickets.
Someone was explaining about off-peak times.
It'd been one of those suddenly hot days
at the end of March and there was something high

and reckless in the air. I'd seen a woman
at the lights with huge long breasts in a low black top
and men with their tongues practically hanging out
and I remember thinking here we go again
and the kids in the back were squabbling and my thighs
sticking together and I wanted only to dive into the pool
though I'd never learnt how and wondered
was it too late and who would I get to teach me?
The road kept on before us, hot and black.
I thought of how big and smooth his face was
as if his features hadn't quite finished forming
though already punched with studs and rings and chains
and his eyes seemed swollen and full of something
like he'd cried a lot as a baby, or not enough.
He never looked at us. I remember thinking
how could this man save us? How would he know
if one of us just stopped and slipped down
on to the tiled floor? He'd look out across
our blue bright shrieking square
but never at us. Not in the way he is now
like the dead do from their crowded lonely stations
and I'm looking at him in a way I never did
when we lived in the same time, same town
with its narrow streets and muck and diesel air.
Now, when he appears there on the pavement,
smoking and squinting in the light, I see
evermoving water, a slab pinned and still,
a body submerged, a body pierced.
But then, when the lights changed and I pulled away
(let me say this now and without pride) I had you
drugged and disaffected, unfucked and aimless
and I marvelled with some bitterness how someone like you
could ever be sleek and forgetful and strong
in the clear blue streams, could ever have the grace
or urge – however vague – to save a life.
How was I to know I'd just seen a man
in his last light, taking time out for a smoke,

a final look at old Fowlers' smashed windows,
its drape of red ivy and dry weeping nests
an hour or so before he swung a leg
over the new bike, dropped the visor down,
wound his way out in the low evening sun
to the A28, the Little Chef bend, the lorry.

Donna Stonecipher

Model City [2]

It was like driving out of your way to visit a model city built next to
an iron ore mine, a paragon of city planning, its well-spaced street-
lamps casting small cones of light upon the darknesses of human life.

*

It was like arriving in the mostly abandoned model city and being unable
to discern the features that make it a model city, for all its features
have been incorporated into other cities, because they were so model.

*

It was like driving down the boarded-up main street of the model city with
your windows down, and suspecting that you have come to the wrong
model city, that the new model city, the right model city, lies far off.

*

It was like standing in a cone of light cast by one of the well-spaced
streetlamps of the wrong model city, mined of all its ideas, its boarded-
up windows hiding long-forgotten aspirations for a model life.

Arundhathi Subramaniam

MY FRIENDS

They're sodden, the lot of them,
leafy, with more than a whiff
of damage,
mottled with history,
dark with grime.

God knows I've wanted them different –
less preoccupied, more jaunty,
less handle-with-care,

more airbrushed,
less prone
to impossible dreams, less perishable,

a little more willing
to soak in the sun.

They don't measure up.
They're unpunctual.
They turn suddenly tuberous.

But they matter
for their crooked smiles,
their endless distractions,
their sudden pauses –

signs that they know
how green stems twist

and thicken
as they vanish
into the dark,

making their way
through their own sticky vernacular tissues
of mud,

improvising,
blundering,
improvising –

George Szirtes

LIKE THAT RAW ENGINE

Like placing a stone
in the dead centre of night,
a hard lightless sun.

Like falling from day
into an electric pool
of unlit currents.

Like horizontal.
Like fish alive on a slab.
Like breathing. Like light.

Like a parallel
existence. Like another.
Like something else here.

Like the rain in dreams
only absent. Like the rain
in life still falling.

Like a distant car
moving towards you. Like that.
Like that raw engine.

Like time in darkness,
undetectable, hanging,
uncertain yet clear.

To sing what is 'like'.
To talk into parallels.
To think like water.

Speak into silence.
Who listens as intently?
Who answers? Who wakes?

And the night opens
its hands and gives you something:
a gift of plain tongues.

Kate Tempest

Thirteen

The boys have football and skate ramps.
They can ride BMX
and play basketball in the courts by the flats until midnight.
The girls have shame.

One day,
when we are grown and we have minds of our own,
we will be kind women, with nice smiles and families and jobs.
And we will sit,
with the weight of our lives and our pain
pushing our bodies down into the bus seats,
and we will see thirteen-year-old girls for what will seem like the first
    time since we've been them,
and they will be sitting in front of us, laughing
into their hands at our shoes or our jackets,
    and rolling their eyes at each other.

While out of the window, in the sunshine,
the boys will be cheering each other on,
and daring each other to jump higher and higher.

Pam Thompson

POSTCARDS FROM BELFAST

Springfield Road

Black cab parked in a street
where Orangemen march. The driver lists
numbers of police, armoured cars. 'Picture',
he says, 'August 15th 1969'. Catholic houses burned, blue
smoke. That house, re-built without windows.
Closed, cold. Turned into ice.

The Crown

Gorgeous, ornate. Tom's Smirnoff Ice,
too sweet, not to my taste. Outside, street
with Union Jack kerbstones. Window
of Wetherstones cracked by a chair. Lists
of football fans' sins ready for the 'papers. Blue,
red, white. Lamp-post, dummy hanging. Harsh picture.

Causeway

Those two. Take a picture.
Giants, who tingled, no doubt, with icy
testosterone fuel, whipped up blue-
black sea, and mad, split streets
of basalt. Be sure to list
it all too. Slam shut its banging window.

Park Hotel

Not stopping by woods but by a window
of a Belfast hotel. Picture
of the night before: smashed-glass, wannabee C-listers
straggling outside clubs; slow ice-
afternoon when dejected Poland fans, street-
sweepers, bus-tour touts, freeze into blue.

Republican Museum

Replica of a cell in Armagh women's jail. Grey-blue
breeze-blocks covered with kids' drawings. No window
yet these *are* windows. In a back street
off the Falls, you'd never find it. Pictures
of hunger-strikers: harps, guitars, carved in the Maze under ice-
glaze display. Tricolor: dead freedom-fighters. Long list.

Shankhill Road

How long did it take him to learn this list
of events; the iconography of murals; to talk this blue
passionate streak, like a mariner rescued from ice-
floes now destined to tell his people's story, wiping the window
of the Troubles, making it easy to picture
the severed hand of Ulster crawling up your street.

Postscript

A weekend's a small window on this list
of must-sees. Wall blocks blue sky, street,
icy gunmetal grey: future's grainy picture.

Jack Underwood

I could go around all evening dropping slices of lime
into other peoples' drinks, because it's easy to give
away fractions of happiness. But bad news ticks
in the kettle as it rests, and someone's dressed
as Death in the Halloween party photo, and
someone's dressed as Death in the birthday
party photo, class photo, front row, by the font
at the Christening… I should've called.
I should've called right away, welcomed your
sadness, taken it, pulled up a white plastic patio
chair, and said *I know you don't want to be here
either*. Instead I let a week pass. It was so easy.

Kate Wakeling

Riddle

And how does it move?
Its fat, blind feet pound my hands.

What does it show you?
Murky gold; a rage; where the dust falls.

How does it conduct the light?
With shaggy beats of its careless head.

Where does it leave the curses?
In the thin waters; at the fireside; where the veins open.

What does it hold?
A casket of blue filament.

What does it wish for?
To heap its rough tongue across dainty machines.

How does its warmth persist?
Through the acute force of the hammer.

When does it march with a sombre tread?
When both the wells are empty.

Where does it sleep?
On my bed like a thief.

Tom Weir

Monsoon

The lightning, diluted by the orange sheet you hung above the
   window,
is the same as the lamp's faint glow that twitches with each shock
   of noise
as each crack of lightning threatens to break the sky.
I don't tell you this isn't normal, that it's never been this bad before;
rain soaking our sheets as it leaks through the ceiling.

I can feel its weight as I make my way across the room where,
above all the noise, I'm not actually sure you ask if everything's
   okay or not
but I tell you it is anyway. You don't need to know about
   the women crying,
the men up to their waists in water, the children held high
above their heads like an offering to a god no one believes in.

Publisher acknowledgements

Natalya Anderson · CLEAR RECENT HISTORY · Bridport Prize

Mona Arshi · THE LION · WHAT EVERY GIRL SHOULD KNOW BEFORE MARRIAGE · *Small Hands* · Part of the Pavilion Poetry series (published by Liverpool University Press)

Sujata Bhatt · POPPIES IN TRANSLATION · *Poppies in Translation* · Carcanet

Kate Bingham · HEELS · *Infragreen* · Seren

Jemma Borg · THE DECORATION · *The Illuminated World* · Eyewear Publishing

Ciaran Carson · IN MEMORY · THE BLOTTING-PAPER · *From Elsewhere* · The Gallery Press

Tom Chivers · SECURITY · *Dark Islands* · Test Centre Publications

Eiléan Ní Chuilleanáin · THE WORDS COLLIDE · DREAM SHINE · *The Boys of Bluehill* · The Gallery Press

Mike Conley · THESE THREE YOUNG LADIES HAVE COME ALL THE WAY FROM AUSTRALIA · *New Welsh Review*

Sarah Corbett · BATH · *And She Was: A Verse-Novel* · Part of the Pavilion Poetry series (published by Liverpool University Press)

Damian Walford Davies · CORPUS · *Judas* · Seren

Maura Dooley · CLEANING JIM DINE'S HEART · *The Poetry Review*

Mark Doty · DEEP LANE · PESCADERO · *Deep Lane* · Cape Poetry

Christy Ducker · SAINT CUTHBERT BANISHES DEMONS FROM THE LASER CLINIC · *Skipper* · smith I doorstop Books

Dan Duggan · DRESSMAKING · *Luxury of the Dispossessed* · Influx Press

Inua Ellams · SHAME IS THE CAPE I WEAR. · Live Canon International Poetry Competition

Andrew Elliott · DOPPELGÄNGER · *Sonofabook*

Steve Ely · THE BATTLE OF BRUNANBURGH: II · *Englaland* · Smokestack Books

Elaine Feinstein · LIFE CLASS: A SKETCH · *Portraits* · Carcanet

Annie Freud · THE JEWELLER · *The Remains* · Picador Poetry

Ann Gray · MY BLUE HEN · *The Moth*

Alan Gillis · BULLETIN FROM THE DAILY MAIL · *Scapegoat* · The Gallery Press

John Glenday · BRITISH PEARLS · *The Golden Mean* · Picador Poetry

Philip Gross · THE PLAYERS · *The Poetry Review*

Padraig Regan · APPLES, CHERRIES, APRICOTS & OTHER FRUITS IN A
    BASKET, WITH PEARS, PLUMS, ROBINS, A WOODPECKER, A PARROT,
    & A MONKEY EATING NUTS ON A TABLE · *The Poetry Review*
Christopher Reid · THE CYCLISTS · *The Curiosities* · Faber & Faber
Peter Riley · DUE NORTH, PART VIII · *Due North* · Shearsman Books
Sam Riviere · AMERICAN SINCERITY · *Kim Kardashian's Marriage* ·
    Faber & Faber
Matthew Siegel · 'FOX GOES TO THE FOX HOSPITAL' · BLOOD WORK ·
    Blood Work · CB editions
Greta Stoddart · LIFEGUARD · *Alive Alive O* · Bloodaxe Books
Donna Stonecipher · MODEL CITY (2) · *Model City* · Shearsman Books
Arundhathi Subramaniam · MY FRIENDS · *When God is a Traveller* ·
    Bloodaxe Books
George Szirtes · LIKE THAT RAW ENGINE · *The Poetry Bus Magazine*
Kim Moore · IN THAT YEAR · *Poetry News*
Kate Tempest · THIRTEEN · *Hold Your Own* · Picador Poetry
Pam Thompson · POSTCARDS FROM BELFAST · Magma Poetry
    Competition
Jack Underwood · AN AVOIDANCE · *Happiness* · Faber & Faber
Kate Wakeling · RIDDLE · *The Rialto*
Tom Weir · MONSOON · *All that Falling* · Templar Poetry
Karen McCarthy Woolf · THE PAPERWORK · THE REGISTRAR'S OFFICE ·
    An Aviary of Small Birds · Carcanet/Oxford Poets

Biographies of the shortlisted writers

Forward Prize for Best Collection

CIARAN CARSON (b. 1948 Belfast) was reared bilingually, Irish being the language of the home and English that of the outside world. As a student at Queen's University, Belfast, he was part of 'The Group' with Seamus Heaney, Michael Longley, Paul Muldoon, Medbh McGuckian and Frank Ormsby. He worked as a musician, in the Civil Service and as a teacher before becoming Professor of Poetry at his alma mater. He won the Forward Prize for Best Collection in 2003 for *Breaking News* (The Gallery Press).

From Elsewhere (The Gallery Press, 2014) is a book of 'translations of translations' from the French poet Jean Follain, each translation faced by the new poem that it inspired. Carson says: 'I wonder how far all this double-dealing comes from my bilingual background, as embodied in my name, Ciaran the Catholic Irish, Carson the Protestant Ulsterman. At any rate I relish the ambiguity.'

EILÉAN NÍ CHUILLEANÁIN (b. 1942 Cork) remembers 'being flabbergasted by the finesse and symmetry of a Shakespeare sonnet' when her mother read to her as a child. She started writing poems seriously when she was 15: 'It was very obscure because I was writing about things I didn't understand. Then, at 20 or so, a poem got published, and I began to realise that if people were to read it, the writing had better be clearer. I still write about things I don't understand, like sex and death and history, but I try to find ways of making them more articulate.'

A translator and editor, as well as a poet, Ní Chuilleanáin has won many literary prizes, including the 2010 Griffin Poetry Prize. She co-founded the literary magazine *Cyphers*, and edited *Poetry Ireland Review*. She is an Emeritus Fellow and Professor of English at Trinity College Dublin.

Her latest collection, *The Boys of Bluehill* (The Gallery Press, 2015), is named after a traditional Irish hornpipe. The *Guardian* recently compared her work 'with her love of dens, hiding-places, ruins and language itself as an in-between space' to that of her compatriot Samuel Beckett. The real drama of *The Boys of Bluehill*, said the reviewer, 'takes place in shadowy, marginal zones'.

Her advice to new poets is: 'Read and keep reading... and definitely never live with anyone who thinks poetry is your hobby.'

PAUL MULDOON (b. 1951 Portadown) first wrote poetry at the age of 13. 'Then, as now, I was fascinated by the power of words to make me see things as if for the first time,' he says. 'A flea. A forest. A fluorescent light.'

While he was still a student at Queen's University, Belfast, his debut poetry collection was published by Faber & Faber. Later accolades include the Pulitzer Prize and the role of Oxford Professor of Poetry, but perhaps the most memorable came early on from Seamus Heaney, to whom the young Muldoon showed a batch of poems with the question: what could be done to improve them? 'Nothing,' Heaney replied.

Since 1987, Muldoon has been a Professor at Princeton University and poetry editor of *The New Yorker*. *One Thousand Thing Worth Knowing* (Faber & Faber, 2015), is his twelfth collection: 'Each time out, it seems as if one might have discovered the source of the Nile,' he says. 'More often than not, it's a septic tank in one's own backyard.'

CLAUDIA RANKINE (b. 1963 Kingston, Jamaica) began writing poems at Williams College, Massachusetts, later deciding against law school to pursue creative writing. 'Being a poet seemed like a risky career choice, but it felt like a calling – I didn't argue.'

Her poetry, plays and criticism have been widely honoured: she is currently a chancellor of the Academy of American Poets and Professor of English at Pomona College, California.

Citizen: An American Lyric (Penguin Books, 2015) may seem at first glance not to be poetry at all but a collage of prose, graphic art, photography and scraps of documentary film script, all centered on the theme of racism. It won the National Book Critics Circle Award for Poetry in America after becoming the first book in the prize's history to be a finalist in both the poetry and criticism categories. The form of the collection, she says, is 'both archival and curatorial'. The much-praised opening sequence, in which a series of un-named speakers tell of racist 'micro-aggressions', came about 'by asking friends to share their stories regarding interactions with either friends or colleagues'.

Although the book's title might suggests it speaks primarily of America, *The Sunday Times* reviewed it as 'one of the most brilliant pieces of writing that will appear in the UK this year', hailing it as 'the book of a generation'.

PETER RILEY (b. 1940 Stockport) first encountered poetry as a child through 'bright schoolteachers introducing us to Eliot and Pound and encouraging exploration, which mostly took place in second-hand bookshops'. He has more than 20 publications to his name, including studies of burial mounds, village carols, lead mines and Transylvanian string bands: the sheer range of his work defies attempts to pigeon-hole him, although it is relatively safe to say that much of his work engages with landscape, often English, but also French, Italian or Transylvanian.

Riley studied at Cambridge, and then at the universities of Keele and Sussex and has taught in Denmark. He subsisted as a bookseller for many years and declares he would rather be known as 'writer' than 'poet'.

Due North (Shearsman Books, 2015) was inspired by his move back to the area of his birth. Its themes are displacement and quest: he worked towards it by gathering a 'great deal of thought, research, note-making and fragmentary passages of poetry concerning movements of populations'.

His advice to young poets is: 'Beware of polemical concepts, which threaten to narrow the poem concept. Get an idea of what you believe in, what a poem by you could be and do it at its best.'

Forward Prize for Best First Collection

MONA ARSHI (b. 1970 London) grew up in Hounslow, the child of Punjabi Sikh parents. She worked for a decade as a lawyer for the human rights charity Liberty, acting on many high-profile cases, including that of the 'right-to-die' campaigner, Diane Pretty.

Her debut collection, *Small Hands* (Liverpool University Press, 2015), was six years in the writing. It features poems in terza rima, ghazals and a ballad: subjects include the loss of her younger brother, who died three years ago. 'Observing the anguish of a family trying to come to terms and survive was a difficult task, but one I felt I had to negotiate, especially if you believe that one of the functions of poetry is to make the unbearable, bearable.'

She rejects the idea that poetry can be appreciated only by certain people. 'It's simply not true. Writers, and poets in particular, are pathologically inquisitive about the physical world around them and poetry is simply the world we live in, translated into language.'

Arshi studied for a Masters in Creative Writing at the University of East Anglia in 2010, won the inaugural Magma Poetry competition in 2011 and was joint winner in 2014 of the Manchester Poetry Prize. Her work is included in *Ten: The New Wave* (Bloodaxe Books, 2014).

SARAH HOWE (b. 1983 Hong Kong) came as a child to England, her father's country, but grew increasingly interested in the history of her mother, who fled China in 1949. She says, for a long time writing poetry was 'under the radar of my official life as a university teacher and literary critic'.

'Strangely, poetry became the place where I explored my Chineseness, something that otherwise had no place in my life – except perhaps for a hankering to go home to my mum's fried noodles.' It is no coincidence, she adds, that she began to write poetry in earnest while on a scholarship to Harvard, 'a period of geographical displacement, when home was far away and imaginary again.'

The poems in her debut collection, *Loop of Jade* (Chatto & Windus, 2015), span a decade. The earliest is inspired by two journeys: her mother's as a baby and her own first trip to the Chinese mainland in 2004. Her 2009 pamphlet, *A Certain Chinese Encyclopedia* (tall-lighthouse), won an Eric Gregory Award, while her poems have appeared widely in magazines and, in 2014, were anthologised in *Ten: The New Wave* (Bloodaxe Books). She is the founding editor of *Prac Crit*, an online journal of poetry and criticism and is a Research Fellow at Gonville and Caius College, Cambridge, where she teaches Renaissance Literature. In 2015-16, she took up a year's writing fellowship at Harvard University's Radcliffe Institute.

ANDREW MCMILLAN (b. 1988 Barnsley) grew up in a house with lots of poetry books and acknowledges Thom Gunn as a major influence: 'the first poet I read who I thought represented something of my own experience'. He describes his debut collection *physical* (Cape Poetry, 2015) as 'a collection about the male gaze on the male body'. He began it in 2008, after breaking up with his first long-term boyfriend: as the collection developed, he found himself creating 'physical, tight, muscular poems which would look unemotionally at things which had happened, and attempt to come to some sort of redemption from them'.

He has published three pamphlets with Red Squirrel Press, *every salt advance* (2009), *the moon is a supporting player* (2011) and *protest of the physical* (2013), and his poems have featured in 2011's *Salt Book of Younger Poets* as well as in *Best British Poetry 2013* (Salt). He was named a 'new voice' in 2012 by both Latitude Festival and Aldeburgh Poetry Festival. McMillan is a lecturer in Creative Writing at Liverpool John Moores University and a writer in residence at the charity First Story.

MATTHEW SIEGEL (b. 1984 New York) knew from the age of 16 that he loved writing poetry more than anything in his life. At the same age, he was diagnosed with Crohn's disease: the struggle to remain whole in the face of his condition is the subject of his debut collection, *Blood Work* (CB editions, 2015).

First published in the USA by the University of Wisconsin Press after the manuscript won the prestigious Felix Pollak Prize, the book was hailed as 'a genuine contribution to the literature of illness' by the poet Mark Doty. He said, 'In Siegel's capable hands, illness reveals how barely contained any human being is, and how we reach, alone and together, for whatever will hold us.'

The poets Siegel most admires are Walt Whitman and Rainer Maria Rilke. His own advice to a young poet is to 'be an active, hungry reader... you have to be willing to not look for reasons to dismiss work too quickly. Be ruthless only with your own truth. Know when you're saying something that isn't true.'

Siegel was a Wallace Stegner Fellow at Stanford University, USA. He currently teaches Literature and Creative Writing at San Francisco Conservatory of Music.

KAREN MCCARTHY WOOLF (b. 1966 London) wrote poetry as a teenager, encouraged by a 'mum who could write rhyming couplets standing on her head', but credits the Forward Prizes with drawing her back to poetry as an adult. She picked up *The Forward Book of Poetry 1995* in a bookshop and read a poem by Kwame Dawes, which left her profoundly moved.

Her debut collection, *An Aviary of Small Birds* (Carcanet/ Oxford Poets, 2014) commemorates the loss of her stillborn son, Otto, in 2009. At the time, she had been working on a collection populated by many other poems but the work she wrote in response to maternal loss 'demanded their place and I wanted to make space for them'.

Her pamphlet, *The Worshipful Company of Pomegranate Slicers* (Spread the Word, 2005), was a *New Statesman* Book of the Year. In 2008, Woolf was one of ten poets selected for The Complete Works – a nationwide mentoring scheme that aims to increase cultural diversity in poetry publishing. She chose as mentor the poet Michael Symmons Roberts, and maintains close links with the scheme, as editor of *Ten: The New Wave* (Bloodaxe Books, 2014), the anthology of Complete Works II poets. She is working towards a PhD at Royal Holloway: her thesis looks at new ways of writing about nature in the face of climate change.

Forward Prize for Best Single Poem

MAURA DOOLEY (b. 1957 Truro) lectures on creative writing at Goldsmiths, University of London, where her students include many skilful and dedicated young poets: the college's reputation as a centre of poetic energy owes much to her work. She is of Irish extraction and studied at the universities of York and Bristol.

Dooley's poetry has been praised for its 'ability to enact and find images for complex feelings' (Adam Thorpe). Two of her poetry collections have been shortlisted for the TS Eliot prize. 'Cleaning Jim Dine's Heart' (*The Poetry Review*) will be published next year in her forthcoming collection with Bloodaxe Books.

Her efforts on behalf of poets and poetry include five years as organiser of creative writing courses for the Arvon Foundation at Lumb Bank in Yorkshire; she was founding director of the Literature series at London's Southbank Centre, creating a year-round programme of talks, fiction and poetry readings and re-establishing, after an absence of 20 years, the major festival *Poetry International*.

Her advice to anyone starting out in poetry today is 'Pay no attention to fashion. Read, read, read: read across centuries, traditions and continents.'

ANDREW ELLIOTT (b. 1961 Limavady) published his first book, *The Creationists*, with Blackstaff Press in 1988. Of his second collection Ciaran Carson wrote, '*Lung Soup* is a tour de force: nearer perhaps to the prose of Thomas Pynchon or Italo Calvino in its play with genre than any I can think of.'

Mortality Rate, a book that moves between the hinterlands of Germany, America and the internet, was published by CB editions in 2013. His poem 'Doppelgänger' was first published in CB editions' *Sonofabook* magazine. He politely declines to share details about himself, his background or his thoughts about poetry.

ANN GRAY (b. 1948 London) trained as a nurse and is based in Cornwall, where she owns a care home for elderly people with dementia. The author of a number of collections including *Painting Skin* (Fatchance Press, 1995) and *The Man I Was Promised* (Headland, 2004), Ann was commended for the National Poetry Competition 2010 and won the Ballymaloe Poetry Prize in 2014. Her studies for an MA in Creative Writing from the University of Plymouth led to her collection of poems about the sudden loss of her partner, *At the Gate* (Headland, 2008). 'My Blue Hen' is one of many written since, which, she says, 'prove' she was not finished with those poems.

It is 'a love song and a spell', inspired by the experience of moving her chickens to a safer place after a fox attack: 'Although I was weeping with fatigue from walking up and down the hill, I found myself singing to the last hen to console her, to console myself.'

CLAIRE HARMAN (b. 1957 Surrey) is best known as a biographer. She began her career in publishing at Carcanet Press and the poetry magazine *PN Review*, where she was co-ordinating editor in the 1980s. Her first book, a life of the writer Sylvia Townsend Warner, was published in 1989 and won the John Llewellyn Rhys Prize. She has since published acclaimed biographies of Fanny Burney and Robert Louis Stevenson and edited works by Stevenson and Warner. *Jane's Fame*, a study of Austen's authorship and reception, was published in 2009 and her new biography of Charlotte Brontë is out in October 2015. She has taught English at the Universities of Manchester and Oxford and Creative Writing at Columbia University in New York.

'The Mighty Hudson' began with a comment from a friend showing her the view over the Hudson river in upstate New York. The phrase 'The Mighty Hudson' intrigued her. 'I thought what a great name for a strong man that would be, and I suppose that and the place names along the drive and the look of the blazing autumn leaves all lodged in my mind somehow.

'The story of the poem emerged quite effortlessly but is entirely made up. I was very impressed by how plausible it seemed, so made up the epigraph from the newspaper – and the newspaper – to give it some actual credibility. And I had a sense of the rhythm before any of the story, even: that long thrumming line seemed to be there in advance, appropriate and anticipatory. There's something inherently deadpan about it.'

KIM MOORE (b. 1981 Leicester) teaches the trumpet to schoolchildren in Cumbria for three days a week and works as a freelance writer the other two. Her first collection *The Art of Falling* was published by Seren in 2015. Her pamphlet *If We Could Speak Like Wolves* was a winner in the 2012 Poetry Business Pamphlet Competition and was shortlisted for the Michael Marks Award and a runner-up in the Lakeland Book of the Year. She was awarded the Geoffrey Dearmer Prize in 2010 and an Eric Gregory Award in 2011.

'In That Year' is part of a sequence of poems which explores domestic violence within a relationship. It is the first poem in the sequence – which forms part of *The Art of Falling*. 'It sets out a lot of the ideas that are explored throughout the rest of the sequence,' she says, highlighting 'the use of animals, birds, insects and the body to explore issues of power and control.'

Previous winners of the Forward Prizes

2005 · Helen Farish · *Intimates* · Cape Poetry
2004 · Leontia Flynn · *These Days* · Cape Poetry
2003 · AB Jackson · *Fire Stations* · Anvil Press
2002 · Tom French · *Touching the Bones* · The Gallery Press
2001 · John Stammers · *Panoramic Lounge-Bar* · Picador Poetry
2000 · Andrew Waterhouse · *In* · The Rialto
1999 · Nick Drake · *The Man in the White Suit* · Bloodaxe Books
1998 · Paul Farley · *The Boy from the Chemist is Here to See You* ·
      Picador Poetry
1997 · Robin Robertson · *A Painted Field* · Picador Poetry
1996 · Kate Clanchy · *Slattern* · Chatto & Windus
1995 · Jane Duran · *Breathe Now, Breathe* · Enitharmon
1994 · Kwame Dawes · *Progeny of Air* · Peepal Tree
1993 · Don Paterson · *Nil Nil* · Faber & Faber
1992 · Simon Armitage · *Kid* · Faber & Faber

Best Single Poem
2014 · Stephen Santus · In a Restaurant · Bridport Prize
2013 · Nick MacKinnon · The Metric System · *The Warwick Review*
2012 · Denise Riley · A Part Song · *London Review of Books*
2011 · RF Langley · To a Nightingale · *London Review of Books*
2010 · Julia Copus · An Easy Passage · *Magma*
2009 · Robin Robertson · At Roane Head · *London Review of Books*
2008 · Don Paterson · Love Poem for Natalie "Tusja" Beridze ·
      The Poetry Review
2007 · Alice Oswald · Dunt · *Poetry London*
2006 · Sean O'Brien · Fantasia on a Theme of James Wright ·
      The Poetry Review
2005 · Paul Farley · Liverpool Disappears for a Billionth of a Second ·
      The North
2004 · Daljit Nagra · Look We Have Coming to Dover! · *The Poetry
      Review*
2003 · Robert Minhinnick · The Fox in the Museum of Wales ·
      Poetry London
2002 · Medbh McGuckian · She Is in the Past, She Has This Grace ·
      The Shop
2001 · Ian Duhig · The Lammas Hireling · National Poetry Competition

2000 · Tessa Biddington · THE DEATH OF DESCARTES · Bridport Prize

1999 · Robert Minhinnick · TWENTY-FIVE LAMENTS FOR IRAQ · *PN Review*

1998 · Sheenagh Pugh · ENVYING OWEN BEATTIE · *New Welsh Review*

1997 · Lavinia Greenlaw · A WORLD WHERE NEWS TRAVELLED SLOWLY · *Times Literary Supplement*

1996 · Kathleen Jamie · THE GRADUATES · *Times Literary Supplement*

1995 · Jenny Joseph · IN HONOUR OF LOVE · *The Rialto*

1994 · Iain Crichton Smith · AUTUMN · *PN Review*

1993 · Vicki Feaver · JUDITH · *Independent on Sunday*

1992 · Jackie Kay · BLACK BOTTOM · Bloodaxe Books

If you would like to know more about the past, present or future of the Forward Prizes for Poetry or become involved with National Poetry Day, please register on our website www.forwardartsfoundation.org